THE PERGAMON ENGLISH LIBRARY

EDITORIAL DIRECTORS: GEORGE ALLEN AND BORIS FORD
EXECUTIVE EDITOR: ESMOR JONES
PUBLISHER: ROBERT MAXWELL, M.C., M.P.

SCOPE: *Spoken Communication as an Open-plan Project in Education*

TO SPEAK TRUE

'The moral my lord is not just to speak, but to speak true'
(SHAKESPEARE, *A Midsummer Night's Dream*)

For John and Michael

TO SPEAK TRUE

BY

BETTY MULCAHY

1966

THE QUEEN'S AWARD
TO INDUSTRY 1966

PERGAMON PRESS

PERGAMON PRESS LTD.

OXFORD · LONDON · EDINBURGH
NEW YORK · TORONTO · SYDNEY

Copyright © 1969 BETTY MULCAHY

*All Rights Reserved. No part of this publication may be
reproduced, stored in a retrieval system, or transmitted, in
any form or by any means, electronic, mechanical, photo-
copying, recording or otherwise, without the prior permission of Pergamon Press Ltd.*

First edition 1969

Library of Congress Catalog Card No. 72–84074

Printed in Great Britain by A. Wheaton & Co., Exeter

08 006444 2

SOCRATES: Your profession, O Ion, has often appeared to me to be an enviable one. For, together with the nicest care of your person, and the most studied elegance of dress, it imposes upon you the necessity of a familiar acquaintance with many and excellent poets. . . . Nor is it merely because you can repeat the verses of this great poet that I envy you, but because you fathom his inmost thoughts. For he is no rhapsodist who does not understand the whole scope and intention of the poet, and is not capable of interpreting it to his audience. This he cannot do without a full comprehension of the meaning of the author he undertakes to illustrate; and worthy, indeed, of envy are those who can fulfil these conditions.

(From: *Five Dialogues* of PLATO. *Ion*, translated by PERCY BYSSHE SHELLEY.)

Contents

Introduction

ALL over the country – in management, in the theatre and in education – there is a growing realisation that the art of speech, as communication to others, needs reassessing and revitalising. In business management this results in courses designed to help reduce tension between workers and managers, offering techniques designed to improve spoken communication. In the theatre actors are taking part in daily classes to improve their vocal techniques – comparable to the limbering exercises of the dancer or the scales of the musician.

In education the endeavour to make spoken English a compulsory subject both in G.C.E. and C.S.E. has emphasised the need for more instruction in the spoken use of language, requiring highly trained teachers. As William Walsh says in his perceptive book, *The Use of Imagination*,

> Language is the one indispensable means of education, both in the stricter sense of formal education, in which stress falls on the communicative function of language, and in the looser sense of incidental education, in which the expressive function of language is emphasised.

The functional use of oral language, now being called 'oracy', will come into the province of the English teachers, who must be trained to accept responsibility for teaching spoken as well as written English, and in this field the recent Newsom Report on Education stated:

> Real communication begins when the words are about experience, ideas, and interests, which are worth putting into language,

and

> Attention should be paid both to the imaginative experience through the arts, and the personal and social development of the pupils.

This suggests rather more than the ability to deliver a short talk or 'lecturette' on a favourite subject; to handle questions from an audience; to give directions clearly and concisely; or to converse with a group of students on a topic of the day – all suggested means of examining oracy. It suggests more than the ability to research and prepare material for a debate or to inform, instruct, or explain a known technique. In fact it suggests that we are nearing the realm of artistic speech, or expressive speech, which requires some skill and craftsmanship.

To read aloud a factual notice or news item requires clarity, projection, and variety. But to read aloud a dramatic passage from a novel and to bring this to life for the listeners must involve all the techniques of vocal modulation allied to imaginative thinking, characterisation, and the power to communicate. It begins to take us into the realm of the actor or orator. Yet the ability to read a prose passage, either prepared or un-prepared, forms part of most suggested forms of oracy examination, and indeed it would seem to be fatal to neglect this valuable source of inspira-tion in training students to be exponents of spoken as well as written English. But though immense time and care are taken in teaching young people to write good prose, little or no attention is paid to teaching them how to read or speak good prose in such a way as to arrest and sustain the attention of the listener. English teachers do not require this knowledge to gain an English degree, and therefore many of them are unable to give this sort of instruction to their students.

In fairness to our educational system it must be said that this apparent void is perhaps a revulsion against the abuse of oral communication perpetrated in the name of 'elocution'. But these malpractices are merci-fully dying out, though the image of hideous artificiality tends to linger. But the theatre, the press, and the mass media of television and radio must take their share of the blame. In their all-out and sentimental rush for phoney 'realism' they have reduced language standards alarmingly, and the cult of pop-idols – their mangled speech hiding the idiocy of many of their so-called 'lyrics – has added to the wreckage. It is difficult to persuade young people that the ability to express themselves in fluent, flexible, and vital language is a desirable asset when their heroes and heroines, earning vast sums of money, can barely put two words together. Yet a further quotation from the Newsom report says:

> There is no gift like the gift of speech; and the level at which people have learned to use it determines the level of their companionship, the level at which their life is lived.

If instruction in reading and speaking prose has been neglected, how much more neglected has been the reading and speaking aloud of poetry. The use of expressive prose as description of character, situation, or action, or as a narrative, develops out of its use for more mundane purposes of reporting, direction, instruction, etc., and therefore its place in the English lesson is quite natural, language and literature forming complementary sections of the whole.

But what of poetry? Is it an art form? If so, would it not be better appreciated if it took its place alongside the other art forms of music, painting, drama, etc., as a recreational subject? Should it not be taught by a specialist? As music, painting, drama? Perhaps a practising poet? Would not this help to give status to both poet and poetry? This may be regarded as hopelessly idealistic in a technological age, but this would appear also to be an age when the arts are flourishing thanks to a more enlightened general educational system and wider opportunities for all members of the community. Many English teachers might be relieved to relinquish the task of presenting poetry to sometimes hostile or indifferent classes. Where the English teacher happened to be a specialist and devotee of poetry, he could still be responsible for its presentation, but as a subject on its own rather than, as so often happens, a 'poor relation' to the main English lesson. After all, it is amazing that in a country which produces more great poets than any other country in the world there is still:

(1) Lack of any recognisable standard of speaking poetry, and therefore of what is possible and can be achieved.
(2) Lack of any informed criticism of public performance.
(3) Lack of any specialised or specific training of speakers or teachers.
(4) Lack of imaginative presentation in theatre, concert hall, or on television.

In educational drama, thanks to such inspired teachers as Peter Slade and Brian Way, there has been a revolution in the whole approach to the subject. No longer the chosen few appearing in the annual school play, but drama for all, with the emphasis on the need of each individual pupil. But though outstanding results have been obtained in the realms of physical freedom and expressive movement, no one would pretend that there has been a corresponding growth of vocal freedom and expressive use of spoken language. Yet language is man's main means of communication, and poetry its supreme achievement.

Why then has there been no corresponding development in the presentation of poetry? I believe this is due to a lack of knowledge of the craft of reading and speaking poetry aloud. As with music, painting, and dance, I believe the teacher should be an exponent of his subject as well as being trained to teach it. There are academies for teaching music, painting, ballet, and drama. There are careers for talented students in these fields, either as performers or teachers. There are no academies for teaching the art of spoken poetry and no careers for performers or teachers. The subject is therefore left to actors and poets in public and to English teachers in the classroom. There are relatively few books to help them, and yet many actors and teachers do sincerely want to communicate better through poetry. When poetry is well spoken and well presented, audiences and classes respond with enthusiasm. Is it hopelessly idealistic to hope that one day a small academy might be formed where eminent teachers and poets could combine in an effort to train a nucleus of speakers who, by the excellence of their programmes, might create an audience for and eventually a career in spoken poetry? There is so much unused talent among teachers and actors, but the plain fact is that many cannot find opportunities of perfecting their art or of hearing examples of excellence.

But it must be made clear that the observations and suggestions for training contained in this book are designed mainly for the specialist teacher or reader and not generally for their pupils. Where the word 'student' is used it is referring to the student-teacher or student-actor who may well be widely experienced in his own field but still be a student of verse-speaking. Then teachers themselves can safely be left to find the best ways of adapting these ideas to suit their particular circumstances and pupils.

To those educationists still wary of letting either junior or senior students read aloud the poems they like or have written themselves there is this to be said. Words are for communication between people. If, from the very earliest age, children are encouraged to share their poems with their class, their teacher, or their parents, they will feel no strain or self-consciousness when doing so. Of course their technical ability is limited, but so it is in the realm of singing, yet no one wishes to prevent the school choir from getting and giving enjoyment through song. Why not through poetry? Naturally some will be more adept than others. But someone is going to win the egg-and-spoon race, yet no one suggests that because of this sports day should be eliminated or that there should be no spectators in case the competitor who comes in last should be discomforted. The superb use of language which our poets provide is every child's inheritance, and the joy of speaking the poet's words should be denied to none.

But the greatest spur to enthusiasm will be the teacher's own example, the hearing of fine recordings, or the experience of poetry in theatre, concert hall, or on television. It is with the sincere hope that something of one person's experience may help others to achieve for poetry speaking the full status it deserves in education and in public performance that this book is offered.

CHAPTER 1

Verse Speaking as an Art Form

> The theory of language most influential today is a theory of the incapacity of language. The elements of the situation are commonly seen to assume a pattern of this sort. On the one hand there is the subject, the interpreting power, intelligence, on the other the object, the material of interpretation, reality, and between them stands the means of interpretation, language, maimed in its origins and radically inadequate for its purpose, and by reason of its coarseness and clumsiness incapable of any but blurred and inaccurate kinds of transmission, of the merest gestures at meaning.
>
> (W. WALSH, *The Use of Imagination.*)

If we accept that language in its origins was onomatopoeic and created from nature and natural surroundings, then it would have grown from rhythmic patterns and in its origins have been nearer to poetry than to prose. Primitive people using the chant accompanied by movement were expressing themselves in sound and sign much as the Greek chorus must have done. Children display the same need when they compose their games and counting rhymes, which are handed down almost unchanged from generation to generation and could form an excellent starting point for an imaginative teacher. A child's first memorised words are invariably rhymes: as Alexander Pope says in his 'Imitations of Horace', 'What will a child learn sooner than a song?' News was originally conveyed in the form of song or ballad, easily remembered and passed on, and modern television advertisements make use of this quality of memorability in their jingles and rhymes. The rhythmic beat of poetry identifies human communication with the permanent rhythm of nature, and this is one of its attractions. Why then does it not hold its rightful place in classroom, concert hall, and theatre? Elizabethan audiences accepted Shakespeare's blank verse with no difficulty, and they were by no means

1

'educated' in the modern sense. Yet as the more 'educated' sections of the population took to theatre-going, so the verse play declined in popularity. Does this not suggest that education is in part responsible for the neglect of the one art form which uses language as imaginative experience and offers real communication, with the words – to quote Newsom again – 'about experience, ideas and interest, which are worth putting into language'?

Why differentiate between the teaching of prose and poetry? While the writing and speaking of good prose is undeniably an art and therefore only partly teachable, it is at least still dealing with a largely 'two-dimensional' use of language. We see (or hear) the words, and we understand what they are saying. Its rhythms consist of the balancing of sentences, the use of climax, the construction of paragraph, etc. It shares many of the devices of poetry, i.e. alliteration, onomatopoeia, metaphor, and simile, etc., and it approaches poetry when it begins to touch the emotions and the senses, and to awaken responses rather than to inform. This is the province of poetic prose. But at its best it is still a heightened and refined form of our own conversations, our own attempts at communication through language. To borrow the words of Leonard Clark: 'Where THINKING comes first associated with FEELING, the words become PROSE; where FEELING comes first associated with THINKING the words tend to become POETRY.'

Thus in spoken prose the speaker has the content, the matter, to impart through his voice, but he does not have that added 'third dimension' which lies just below the surface of all true poetry. This requires more of the speaker or reader, and more, too, of the listener, and therefore a different atmosphere of presentation if its peculiar merits are to be absorbed and appreciated. It seeks to communicate the frequently undefinable – rather as music does – although music is far less specific than poetry. But whereas there is a tradition of musical performance in this country – vast numbers of concerts both live and on radio and television, informed criticism by experts, and the subject taught as a recreation with pupils encouraged to participate, interpret, and listen – poetry is still largely neglected other than as an examination question in the literature paper. Would music have attained its present status if it had merely been presented in schools as an adjunct to drama or a background to dance? Hardly. Examinations in music are reserved for those preparing to specialise or perform. Many non-specialists would lose their enthusiasm for music if forced to answer examination questions on the subject. Yet poetry is forced into this unnatural position by its inclusion in the formal English lesson, and generation after generation of young people leave school and never read a line of poetry again. Few reject all music in this way, and in the realm of the visual arts, though attendance at galleries is still poor, sales of reproductions and, indeed, of original paintings has never been higher, which suggests that the teaching of art is in a very healthy state. The climate is changing, and in the past few years there have been some developments in the teaching of poetry, but until it attains full status as a subject on its own, and an examination subject only to those wishing to specialise, the change must be slow.

To revert once more to the subject of the English teacher. He may well have a special talent for the subject and be an inspired guide, but this is not always the case, and it should not be assumed. It can also be the case – and any English examination paper will bear this out – that the academic approach will kill rather than stimulate interest. Why is this?

Susanne Langer in her book *Feeling and Form* says, 'The import of a poem is lost in a prose paraphrase.' If the 'import' of the poem is emotional – and this is surely true of the majority of poems – then it cannot be reduced to intellectual rationalising without its essential core being lost, and it is this core which is likely to appeal to developing young minds and emotions. This must also widen its appeal, since emotions in varying degrees are common to us all, whatever our intellectual capabilities. The specialist English teacher, through an intimate knowledge of prosody, can begin to regard the whole business as an intellectual exercise. Close familiarity with the craft of the poet can easily blunt the sensibilities to the emotional essence of the poem. As Charles Davy says in his perceptive book *Words in the Mind*, 'studying the menu becomes so absorbing that one forgets to eat!' To offer another analogy. A perfume is made up of many substances crushed together to release their combined essences. One does not need to know these substances to be able to appreciate and enjoy the resulting scent – indeed, to know the substances would in many cases deter purchase. The manufacturer (poet) needs to know these substances. The salesman or teacher must know them too, but in his selling he must only present enthusiasm for the end product or the purchaser (pupil) may well be literally 'blinded by science'. Once interest has been aroused there may well be inquiry, but the poem's 'import' will have been preserved.

In defence of English teachers it must be remembered that many of them have no technique for reading poetry aloud to their class. This can be very inhibiting indeed, and to present deeply emotional poetry to an unresponsive or even hostile group can be agonising. Many ignore the sound of poetry altogether, or in the primary stages settle for narrative or humorous verse instead of the more taxing lyric. Because of these factors and the ever-present examination syllabus, poetry as communication between people is being neglected in the classroom and rejected in adult life. Yet it is surely as communication that its main function lies.

If poetry is an art form, what is its task in society? Frederick Grubb in his book *A Vision of Reality* says:

> Art's task is not to tell man whence he came and whither he is going, *why* he is; art's task is to tell man *how* he is in the light (or darkness) of what he has been, and to suggest through revelation and criticism what he may become.

Sigmund Freud says:

> Aesthetic pleasure might be interpreted as a kind of bait whereby we are enticed into letting a work of art bring about in us the same kind of emotional release which the creation of it provided for the artist.

This has been called 'emotional escapism', the psychological reason why in the heat of battle or the agony of grief, the ecstasy of joy or the desolation of loneliness, repeated fragments of poems and/or prayers can give comfort and relief. It is further said that the arts can encourage self-indulgence and cause us to neglect social duties by providing a dream world of fantasy instead of the real world of fact. But the arts can and frequently do provide the necessary strength and example of excellence to enable us to carry on with our more mundane social duties. They can provide just the necessary 'uplift' of the spirit which, while present in the actual world, requires the artist to illuminate it. This is not to say that they will sentimentalise the real world, but the artist in society frequently has the gift to see 'sermons in stones and good in everything'. The tragedy is when the artist in society attempts to outdo actuality – to present fictional horror on top of the horrors of which we are all too aware, and then to claim that it is done to shock us into awareness. This is just one of the hazards of the so-called affluent society, and results in the stepping up of horror films, 'theatres of cruelty', and 'sick' poetry which replace the horrors of poverty and hunger still widely experienced in underdeveloped countries.

But the fact remains that even if the arts are used as escape, in poetry at least it is an escape which unites the escaper with another's sufferings or joy as expressed in the poem; an apparently closer identification than could be possible with a known human being because the poet uses language in a way not given to the majority of humanity. For some people poetry, because it uses language, takes them nearer to the heart of the poet than paint can ever take them to the painter or music to the composer. On the other hand, many devoted to music or the visual arts find little pleasure in poetry even when it is enthusiastically presented. One cannot expect 100 per cent conversion to any one art. It depends upon one's need and one's capacity. But a work of art can 'speak' to us, and a poem falls into this category. We can feel it has a message for us. Perhaps if a poem 'strikes a chord' in only one other human being, it can therefore claim to be a work of art, since its purpose of communication has been fulfilled.

So we identify with those given the power to express, and this is therefore the point – communication: but communication of that which lies below the surface of conscious thought into the realms reached by music and by painting, sometimes by dance where the 'poetry of motion' stirs unexplored depths, and lately by prose drama, notably in the so-called Theatre of the Absurd. Playwrights concerned in this movement, e.g. Beckett, Ionesco, Genet, Pinter, and Albee, attempt in their various ways to transmit experience unhindered by story or conclusion much as a poet does. In their case, however, they tend to take everyday colloquial language and, by imposing upon it an order and a pattern, give it the extra dimension which makes it comparable with poetry. After all, the nearer a play becomes to a poem the more difficult it is to say what it is about.

Thus it is the poet in society who overcomes the 'incapacity of language' and arouses our deepest feelings – feeling leading to thinking. 'What passions cannot music raise or quell,' said Dryden. So, surely with poetry. This is really its main function. Not to teach or critically examine or discuss, or even really to describe – though it can do this brilliantly – but to illuminate. To give us the satisfaction of not being alone in our doubts and conflicts, and sometimes to lighten the burden of our human condition. As Eugene Ionesco said:

> I am not alone in the world, as each one of us, in the depths of his being, is at the same time everyone else – my dreams and desires, my anguish and my obsessions do not belong to myself alone; they are part of the heritage of my ancestors, a very ancient deposit to which all mankind may lay claim.

As mentioned earlier, the power to describe with imagination and accuracy comes also into the field of poetic prose where it begins to awaken our sense of imaginative sight, and many prose works by poets have this added dimension of the poet's 'seeing eye'. Plays written by poets frequently penetrate into these regions, and for that reason are sometimes misunderstood, e.g. T. S. Eliot's *The Family Reunion*. One reason at least for the relative failure of this play is that it has seldom been produced for what it is, a three-act poem shared between several speakers who would require months of concentrated rehearsal to be able to achieve the overall harmony of delivery required while preserving the necessary contrasts. But, then, has any director ever had a cast of suitably trained speakers at his disposal? For whereas all will agree that the first priority of the cast of an opera is that they shall be able to sing – closely followed in these days by their ability to act: in ballet the cast must first dance and then act: to suggest that a verse play needs first a cast that can speak verse and then through the verse form can act calls forth scorn and derision. However, some established companies are now holding daily classes in the speaking of blank verse before production of Shakespeare's plays, and the improvement in clarity and depth of meaning is tremendous, though not nearly enough critical acclaim has greeted their efforts. This is no doubt because the large majority of the audience was unaware of the defect and therefore unappreciative of the improvement.

This must occasion some consideration of the audience for poetry (though a later chapter will deal more fully with the subject). In these days of background music, radio and television we have to reaccustom ourselves to actual listening, and our response to poetry must differ from the response which attends on prose. Leaving aside the already-mentioned Theatre of the Absurd, the audience at a prose play knows that they are going to be told something, given facts – either about the situation at the beginning of the play (the exposition), and/or about the characters involved. Then the characters begin to reveal themselves through their prose dialogue, and action and re-action result. Thereon depths of character, inner feelings, emotional responses, etc., are revealed in language which is a heightened form of daily conversation.

But when listening to poetry or to a verse play the 'third dimension' is soon apparent. The sound and arrangement of words is conditioning their overall meaning. It is no longer possible to follow each individual phrase and, as it were, immediately translate into the mind exactly what is meant. This must be a contributory cause of the unpopularity of poetry. The audience prepared for such deep emotional involvement would seem to be in a minority.

There is, of course, the kind of audience quite prepared to listen in a soporific state and merely let the rhythmic sound of the poetry wash over them. They are sometimes the so-called 'poetry lovers' who use poetry as a sort of mass tranquilliser.

At the other end of the scale there were the young enthusiasts who packed the Albert Hall in their thousands and responded somewhat hysterically to the almost tribal dance atmosphere which resulted. In the Liverpool area there is great enthusiasm for poems read to guitar music, though the 'poems' are mostly in the category of extended 'pop' lyrics. These experiments must be welcomed, but there is a danger that primitive language sound *en masse* will produce only primitive and largely physical response.

Yet between these extremes is the whole area of poetic language which can create, extend, and stimulate emotional response, and discipline it by intellectual satisfaction.

Without adequate preparation in education it is small wonder that verse plays and poetry recitals have only limited success. The audience is unaccustomed to hearing language used in this way. It does not respond to actual meaning, begins to distrust, and ultimately to reject. This is not what language is expected to do, and therefore the audience does not really know how to respond. Thus the best audiences for poetry are the truly simple and unprejudiced or the very highly educated – and there are few of either. The vast half-educated mass will generally prefer prose because education has left them unprepared for the somewhat more taxing task of listening to poetry.

The blame for this cannot be put upon the teachers but upon the social situation which forces them to teach facts in order that pupils may pass examinations, presumably to get better jobs with greater opportunity for relaxation. There is, alas, no time to teach them how to enjoy that relaxation once they have acquired it. The irony is that the best work in this field is being done in schools less geared to producing candidates for high-class jobs, who will have insufficient opportunity, money, or time to develop the interest inculcated by their schools. As Frederick Grubb (*op. cit.*) says: 'Material progress is not an idol to be worshipped in barbaric anarchy, but a means to the increase of leisure for the cultivation of ends.'

One must be educated to the arts as to anything else, and this takes time. Appreciation of music, painting, drama, or poetry does not happen by accident, though, because it is one of the basic human needs, exceptional people there will always be who are entirely self-educated in this field. But in education it is surely dangerous to ignore this human need if we are hoping to build a healthy society.

To summarise so far. There are areas of ourselves and of the whole human condition which are explored by the poets and yet are unintelligible to the vast majority of people. Thus though poetic prose may give them pleasure, it will still not reach those areas of response best served by the poets since these are the areas from which poetry emerges. Therefore to regard poetry as primarily an intellectual exercise must be to mistake its fundamental purpose.

Would this seem to remove, say, *The Essay on Man* from the realms of great poetry? It is certainly an 'intellectual exercise', but much much more. Only consider one of the best-known and most widely misquoted phrases in the language:

> A little learning is a dangerous thing,
> Drink deep or taste not the emperean spring.
>
> (ALEXANDER POPE.)

> Know then thyself, presume not God to scan,
> The proper study of Mankind, is Man.
>
> (ALEXANDER POPE.)

Is it not a fact that these couplets are remembered as much for their inevitable rhythmic perfection as for any intellectual content? Similarly with another popular quotation:

> What is this life if, full of care,
> We have no time to stand and stare.
>
> (W. H. DAVIES, 'Leisure'.)

Those who quote invariably add the false stresses which suggest that sound rather than sense is their guiding factor:

> What ís this lífe if, fúll of cáre,
> We háve no tíme to stánd and stáre.

Does knowledge of this couplet modify their lives in any way? Do they take 10 minutes out of every day for quiet meditation? Do they ever read the rest of the poems? Or does the mere repetition of these few words, so harmoniously gathered together, give them the same sort of satisfaction that the mumbling together of the Lord's Prayer can give to congregations who have long since ceased to think of its actual meaning? If so, we may say with Thomas Campion:

> Parrots so can learn to prate
> Our speech by pieces gleaning.

The right sort of presentation in schools, and the final expulsion of the 'learning by rote' or as punishment, should remove this danger.

Is poetry of any use in this scientific age? Religion is frequently being challenged by scientific fact. So, too, is some of the poetry of the past, which can appear naïve in the light of modern discovery. But a great poem tells a truth which is timeless, e.g.:

> Stone walls do *not* a prison make
> Nor iron bars a cage.

> A thing of beauty *is* a joy for ever.* [*My italics.*]

These are truths for all time come hell or fall-out, and while modern poetry, if it is to stand the test of time, cannot ignore scientific truths any more than it can ignore moral ones, the great poets seem to have this knowledge by instinct, and this gives the timeless quality to their work. Shakespeare's knowledge of basic psychology came long before Freud. Understanding of human nature can exist without scientific fact, which merely gives a rational explanation of what has already been apprehended. Thus though the imagery by which these truths are sometimes expressed must constantly be changing in line with modern knowledge, the truths are constant.

Much poetic imagery was, and still is, derived from Nature, e.g. the recurrence of the seasons, the climatic conditions, 'sun and stars', 'wind and waves', and these are likened to human moods, as in the early beginnings of language:

> Passions of rain or moods in falling snow
>
>   (WALLACE STEVENS, 'Sunday Morning'.)

But though soft landings on the moon may change the imagery, it will not obviate the need for poetry or the need for religion of some kind. Indeed, it makes it more than ever necessary. New discoveries can and do increase bewilderment, not lessen it, and in our bewilderment we are relieved to

---

* I am not, of course, suggesting that this is the way to speak the line, but merely emphasising the truth of the statement.

find better minds and the poet's seeing eye cast over these areas as well as over the more familiar ones.

Thus poetry enhances and pinpoints the vague feelings we may have, and satisfies because it relates our possibly uncommunicated fears or joys with those of another human being. This may well be why poetry so often has a greater appeal to the lonely, the outcast, and the social misfit. Out of their deep needs they have appreciated its communicative powers, but if properly presented it will not be limited to the few. It can and should have a much wider appeal once it loses its esoteric image and takes its place among the recognised art forms in education as an expression of human feeling.

This might also have the effect of ridding it for all time of the label of effeminacy. How this can have come about is astonishing, but biographies of poets often tell the mournful tale of their poetic gifts being despised during their schooldays, and even today it is possible to hear the claim that 'boys do not like poetry' – the inference being that they are far too 'masculine' to bother with it. This attitude may have started with Victorian sentimentality and perhaps continued into the twentieth century with the Georgians. There is no doubt, too, that the appallingly low standard of poetry 'recital', the desperate artificiality of delivery, played its part in bringing about this unfortunate state of affairs. Musical evenings and home-made entertainments encouraged the amateur approach to both music and poetry. Music has survived these abuses, but poetry is only just recovering from the recitations which were, and still sometimes are, inflicted upon it.

But to return to Poetic Imagery; it is interesting to consider that 'Nature' poetry can well depend upon the part of the world in which one finds oneself. Nature in England is comparatively gentle and temperate, and has therefore acted as:

> The guide, the guardian of my heart, and soul
> Of all my moral being.
>
> (WORDSWORTH, 'Tintern Abbey'.)

Among hurricanes, typhoons, and tempests would one feel so? A modern production of *As You Like It* had the famous speech of the exiled duke on the subject of the open-air life in an English winter being preferable to the flattery of the court, spoken against a mocking chorus which suggested just the opposite. Yet the truth remains. The calming effect of the English countryside still exists, though one might well hesitate to camp out all the year round. There is, of course, a stability about our landscape which is absent from human frailty, and we tend to turn to something upon which we can depend when our own species have proved unkind. As Wallace Stevens says in 'Sunday Morning',

> There is not any haunt of prophesy
> Nor any old chimera of the grave
> . . . That has endured
> As April's green endures.

Upon this we can depend.

But Science *versus* Poetry need not concern the interpreter since the speaker will see, or attempt to see, what the poet saw and will accept his imagery however unusual or bizarre. The artist in society must always be ahead in his thinking, and a healthy society needs artists to lead them along the paths to greater fulfilment and not to decadence and decay.

Subject matter in poetry has undergone great changes in this century. Yet, like all freedoms, this has dangers. Language can be more direct and yet less meaningful once all is revealed. In an age of amateur as well as professional psychology, many poems read more like case histories. As Leonard Clark says in his article 'Ideas in poetry' (*Poetry Review*, Autumn, 1964):

> With the disappearance of many old ideals and former certainties, there have appeared, not new ideals so much, but new ideas about the workings of the human mind, about personal frustrations and disillusionments, about the intimate relationships between the sexes.

These subjects have always been there, but as a part of life, not, as it sometimes seems nowadays, as the whole. Personal feelings need to be subordinated to wider considerations, to the whole of humanity. Perhaps the poet's seeing eye is becoming too introspective? There is little doubt that the wide cult of 'pop' music, which some educationists see as an alternative to poetry, may have an unhealthy effect since it provides emotional stimulus without intellectual satisfaction. There is therefore a need to provide an alternative stimulus which can offer emotional release combined with intellectual satisfaction, or vice versa, since the very intelligent student may well find his emotional release through initial intellectual delight. It is therefore a task for the teacher to satisfy this need and not neglect it.

The greatest spur to any class will be the teacher's own enthusiasm and example of reading. While he cannot be expected to be a 'star' performer, he can and should be a good demonstrator. There is no doubt that, while the arts of creation and interpretation have much in common with the art of teaching, they are not the same thing and do not always work harmoniously together. Shaw's remark that 'those who can, do, and those who can't, teach', is far from being the whole truth. He might have reversed it to 'those that can't teach, perform', yet every performer is some sort of teacher, and every teacher some sort of performer. But the arts of teaching and performing are different though related, and they need separate study. If the English teacher is going to present poetry he must learn to read it aloud with some mastery of its techniques, and if the actor in verse plays or recitals is going to move audiences, he must treat this art as a special branch of his training. Ezra Pound says, in *Pavannes and Divisions*, 'I believe in technique as a measure of a man's sincerity', and indeed without it success will be very limited. If poetry is read as it deserves to be read, an audience will respond – in part or in whole according to the chosen material, and the needs and capacities of the listeners. (See Chapter 8, Preparation of Programmes.) If there is no success, blame must lie with the exponents and not with the art form itself. A straight 'reading' is rarely enough. It does not illuminate, but frequently confuses and leaves the listener longing for prose. If rhythm, shape, form, and phrasing are not adhered to, as in music, then the resultant speaking merely sounds like over-written prose.

T. S. Eliot says: 'The emotion of art is impersonal, and the Poet cannot reach this impersonality without surrendering himself wholly to the work to be done.' Likewise the speaker.

How does he approach this task?

CHAPTER 2

Preparation of the Poem and Poet

Poetry, which is an unusually heightened form of the language of men, deceives us if we are persuaded that it is the language of Gods.

(W. WALSH, *The Use of Imagination.*)

It is also, surely, mistaken 'idolatry' to imagine a poet unlike ordinary men. His unusualness lies in his ability to put into language his innermost thoughts and feelings. Often, perhaps invariably, these are caused by quite commonplace emotions or occurrences. This recalls the late L. A. G. Strong who, when asked by a rather pretentious lady for the genesis of a lyric poem, replied: 'Madam, I wrote it when I was madly in love with the girl in Boots.' Keats's unrequited love for Fanny Brawne and his poor physical condition were the spur to many of his finest lyrics. Similarly Yeats's unsatisfied love for Maud Gonne, Wordsworth's developing love for nature, Tennyson's grief for his dead friend, John Clare's social isolation – all are common in varying degrees to all humanity. The poet can illuminate by language and this can cause confusion, as the language is thought to be the man. To quote William Walsh again:

> Through language feeling is clarified by thought, and through language, thought is energised by feeling.
>
> Genius is not a uniquely different form of humanity, but rather a finer and fuller organisation of it.

This confusion of 'language' with 'man' has been the part cause of some inability to believe that the man Shakespeare wrote the plays. Though we do well to retain our wonder in the poetry that this one man wrought, the fact that he was 'a man amongst men' must surely increase – not diminish – our amazement. Confusion of language with man is also responsible for the disillusion and disappointment felt by many upon encountering the

14

artist in person. There is the feeling that he is so ordinary in appearance, manner, conversation, sometimes even when talking on his own subject. He may well be greedy, self-indulgent, mean, pompous or self-mocking, ill-mannered or suave, or even drunk and disorderly. We may be led to believe that the best of him goes into his work but does not modify his remaining self to any great degree. But should it? A psychiatrist is not necessarily the most balanced member of society, nor the judge the most wise, although their respective professions might suggest that they should be. They are presumably wise and balanced only in their professional capacities, and one imagines most poets would rather be judged by their poetry than by their public personality.

But it is a fact that close study of the work of a great artist, depth of probing into possible, and often impossible, significances, can and frequently does lead to over-reverence on the part of some teachers which can have the effect of alienating students from the artist as a man. This is particularly unfortunate during the adolescent period and among those of less than first-class intelligence, and it does account in part for the unpopularity of poetry in these spheres. It is just at this stage that poetry can be helpful in solving some of the emotional problems of this difficult period of growth. This strengthens the case for the poet as teacher, because as a practitioner himself he will demonstrate the essentially human quality of all poets and avoid the alienating effect of the over-reverence already referred to. Interest in the subject is always enormously stimulated by the living poet visiting the school to read his own poetry, and most poets are only too ready to do this.

But a poem will extend, as well as mirror, our own experiences. Thus through poetry young people can be helped to mature emotionally as well as to live more fully, surely two of the most important facets of education. Finally, through the speaking of poetry they can learn self-discipline and the ability to enter imaginatively into the thoughts, ideas, and language of others. Paul Valery in *Reflection on Art* says:

> All the artist can do is to fashion some thing that will produce a certain effect on someone's mind. There will never be any accurate way of comparing what has happened in the two minds, and moreover, if what has happened in the one

were communicated directly to the other, all art would collapse, all the effects
of art would disappear. The whole effect of art, the effort the author's work
demands of the consumer, would be impossible without the demands of the
interposition between the author and his audience, of a new and impenetrable
element capable of acting upon other men's being. A creator is one who makes
others create.

If it is true that 'a creator is one who makes others create' then every
speaking of a poem is an act of creation, and this is partly true.

In the early stages the student-speaker will invariably have greater
success in speaking a poem which seems to mirror his own experience.
Possibly while speaking it he will re-experience through imagination his
own remembered emotion. This will give the speaking a validity and
sincerity which will be pleasing and have some reality for the listener. In
early student work this seems an entirely satisfactory way of working. The
chosen poem probably contains a very generalised experience. Expressed
with simplicity and illuminated in the speaking by the speaker's own
associated imagination, the 'new and impenetrable element' mentioned by
Valery occurs. An example of such a poem might be 'Arabia' by Walter
de la Mare.

A student who had spoken this poem with apparently deep recollection
and just the requisite tone of wistful nostalgia was asked whether in fact
she had ever been to Arabia. She admitted that her actual recollection had
been of a recent holiday in Spain. The tone of her voice was warm, there
was a feeling for richness and of colour and contrast, for unusual sights
and sounds, and the speaking had the refreshing naturalness so often lacking when the mouthing of unfamiliar and highly charged poetic language
can often produce an artificial sound if the speaking is not supported by
clear and exact thinking. So far, so good. An experience has been communicated from the poet to the speaker, and a similar – though not
exact – experience has been communicated from the speaker to the listener.
Her powers of imaginative recollection have been extended through the
poet's more skilful use of language. Her own memories have been
sharpened and given a shape and form, and her daily vocabulary enriched.
The nostalgic tone of poet and speaker combined may have given the
listeners a recollection also, have perhaps opened up avenues of thought

otherwise lying dormant. Thus a dead poet, a young girl, and a mixed assembly of people listening have all been united for one brief moment into a shared emotional experience which is unlike that produced by any other medium.

There is a vast mass of poetry of this calibre which is admirably suited to this stage of speaking. It is not the purpose of this book to offer suggestions for material because it is so dangerous to generalise, but it is perhaps relevant to say that this particular poet does have a great appeal to speakers of all ages who are beginning to learn to speak poetry. Perhaps this is because his poems are so well balanced between fact and fantasy and have the sort of twilight atmosphere which exists in the halfway house of learning or in the process of growing up, whether in the actual, technical, or imaginative sense. Technically, too, the poems are well within the scope of apprentice work while at the same time extending enough to prepare speakers for the more complex poems to come. Finally, the language is revelatory and yet simple, and the subjects timeless and untouched by fashion, i.e. nostalgia, mystery, magic, and a gentle sadness, which is a tone quite naturally adopted by most beginners and frequently a result of lack of confidence. However, the successful speaking of one poem is the finest confidence builder of all, so this should be no deterrent. To succeed, even in a small degree, is so much more helpful than to fail, however gloriously, and verse speaking might well be a more popular art form if speakers would only scale their choice of material to their technical ability and emotional development. It is always monstrous to hear carefree young speakers lisping their way happily through Milton's 'On his Blindness' or Donne's 'Batter my Heart'.

To repeat: if only speakers would scale their choice of material to their technical ability and emotional development. Perhaps here we come to the crux of the matter. No pianist would attempt to play a Brahms concerto in the first few terms of learning, yet it is a fact that novice speakers have no such qualms or inhibitions when it comes to choosing poems. For this some of the Drama Academy speech boards and festival organisers must bear blame, though no one can envy them their immeasurably difficult task. Again it is hopeless to generalise, but it is unfortunately true that technical ability does not always go hand in hand with emotional or intellectual maturity, or vice versa, and teachers have to be constantly guarding against letting technically competent speakers speak a poem for which they are just not ready. If the speaker is intellectually and emotionally mature yet technically uncertain, this is much less offensive, since what will be, at least, partially communicated will be the poet's true purpose. The listeners may well be led to reading the poem for themselves afterwards since interest in the poem will have been aroused. But the technically accomplished speaker, who has been unable to encompass the poem's essence, will merely be demonstrating his own cleverness, and this is much less acceptable. It happens frequently with young actors who are overdeveloped vocally and underdeveloped intellectually or have not appreciated that here they are being called upon to 'characterise' in actuality rather than in imagination.

This brings us to the second part of the verse speaker's art, which should make an immediate appeal to the actor and render him not the least but the most successful speaker of poetry. For it is now that the really fascinating part of the art begins. To requote Valery once more: 'A creator is one who makes others create.' Speaking poetry can therefore be likened to an act of creation in the first stages. So the young girl 'created' her own remembered experience through the poem of Walter de la Mare. But if we now look at a rather different situation, using a poem of John Clare, we may see that this is indeed only half the story.

The Frightened Ploughman
by JOHN CLARE

I went in the fields with the leisure I got;
The stranger might smile but I heeded him not;
The hovel was ready to screen from a shower,
And the book in my pocket was read in an hour.

The bird came for shelter, but soon flew away;
The horse came to look, and seemed happy to stay;
He stood up in quiet, and hung down his head,
And seemed to be hearing the poem I read.

The ploughman would turn from his plough in the day
And wonder what being had come in his way,
To lie on a mole-hill and read the day long
And laugh out aloud when he'd finished his song.

The peewit turned over and stooped o'er my head
Where the raven croaked aloud like the ploughman ill-bred,
But the lark high above charmed me all the day long,
So I sat down and joined in the chorus of song.

The foolhardy ploughman I well could endure;
His praise was worth nothing, his censure was poor;
Fame bade me go on, and I toiled the day long,
Till the fields where he lived should be known in my song.

On the face of it the student will see that this is a quiet lyric, written in four-line stanzas, having almost a tripping four-beat rhythmic line. Its content suggests a young man taking a day off to lie in a field, observe nature, and write a poem. Some might argue that spoken simply and sincerely like this it could succeed. But a sensitive speaker may well find a sense of isolation develops in the speaking of this poem, occasioned by the choice of words, and certainly by the title – 'The Frightened Ploughman'. Why the word 'Frightened'? Phrases like 'The stranger might smile but I heeded him not'. Surely this was no ordinary country lad; to read a book in an hour – to read aloud a poem to a horse – to laugh aloud – to join in singing with the birds – to write a poem? He was certainly superior in intellect to the peasant ploughman, viz. 'The foolhardy ploughman I well could endure; / His praise was worth nothing, his censure was poor.' His opinions apparently counted for nothing, and his manners were 'ill-bred'. 'Fame' had already come and was beckoning the poet to further effort, and so he 'toiled the day long' to describe the countryside in his poem. All this will suggest the isolation of this one human being on this particular day, and from the poem will emerge something of the character of the poet himself. If the speaker is sensitive and imaginative a complete and viable interpretation of the poem will ultimately arrive. But in the intermediate stages some study of the poet's life may help the process. This is not to suggest that a poem is necessarily autobiographical, or that a good poem cannot stand on its own merits, but just as a friend's actions or remarks can be interpreted better through our knowledge of his character, and misunderstanding sometimes avoided, so our arrival at a poem's inner heart may be assisted by some knowledge of its maker. As Helen Gardner says in *Business of Criticism*:

> A poem is not what I choose to make of it. It is something which its author made with deliberation, choosing that it should say this and not that. . . . He may not have known all that he meant to say when he began; but some conception, either clearly formed before he began to write, or growing as he wrote, governed his creation, so that the final poem had unity of thought, feeling, rhythm and diction.

The sad life of John Clare was occasioned by his gift for writing poetry. Had he been content to be a farm labourer, to marry and have children, and to die, that would have been that.

> Man comes and tills the field and lies beneath,
> And after many a summer dies the swan.
>
> (TENNYSON, 'Tithonus'.)

But he needed desperately to express himself in language, and his early success encouraged and, it is to be hoped, sustained him even when his mental and physical health broke down under the severe privations he endured. Reading the poem only will give a feeling of isolation and loneliness. Knowledge of Clare's mental breakdowns and of the kind of asylum to which he would have been committed will surely deepen appreciation of his feelings on this day spent among the kindlier creatures of the fields and skies. The horse did not laugh at him, but his own seemingly 'mad' laughter frightened the ploughman, who must have been alarmed to discover one of the asylum inmates in his field. To anyone who knew anything at all about John Clare (and should anyone speak any poet without knowing something about him, assuming his identity is known?) the speaking of this poem as a straight lyric would be incomplete. Therefore the speaker has to endeavour, through his speaking, to find the very soul of John Clare. He is now thinking not his own thoughts but those of the poet. Thought and speech must become one. This is now interpretation, not creation.

But the vexed question is, How near to the poet's actual voice must the speaker get? Clare no doubt used a Northampton dialect, though there is little hint of this in the writing. Must this poem be spoken by a man, since Clare was a man? Can male poets only be spoken by men and women poets by women? How far does any true poem transcend its maker and become a separate entity capable of being interpreted in numerous different ways?

These and many related questions are dealt with by Francis Berry in his fascinating book *Poetry and the Physical Voice*, and the reader is urged to read all that Berry has to say upon the subject without delay. But though many questions are posed, we are still left in some doubt as to how to proceed. These questions are almost impossible to answer, but it is hoped that the following summary of one person's experience may be helpful.

Human voices are as individual as human finger-prints and no two can ever be exactly alike. Thus to the poet's original 'voice' as 'heard' from the page is added that of the speaker. He will be endeavouring with all sincerity to reproduce what he has 'heard' from the page, but he must unconsciously add some quality of his own. This may well subtract from the poem's worth, and in unsuccessful speaking this is exactly what it does, or it may provide an extra dimension not necessarily intended by the poet, but equally not necessarily irrelevant to the poem's purpose. As the poet Jon Silkin said on the subject of writing poetry, the poet prepares one area of ground, rather as a farmer prepares a field. Into this area he will sow certain seeds. He hopes they will grow. What he cannot know is how many other plants may appear within the prepared area, and whether by cross-fertilisation they may not improve the final crop.

This fascinating study of finding the poet's voice can be compared to the most subtle form of characterisation, and hence the possibility of its appeal to the actor. It is surely as interesting, if not vastly more interesting, to study an actual person as it is to study a fictitious character such as Hamlet, Lear, or Othello. In recent times we have had the astonishing luck to see Othello played by two of our leading actors, Sir John Gielgud and Sir Laurence Olivier. Both, we may be sure, gave intense and careful study to the part, searching as an actor must to find the 'man' behind the text. Yet each produced a totally different result. In general terms Sir John gave us the maturity, the father-figure, the protectiveness, and aristocracy of the Moor without his sexuality and deep physical involvement, and Sir Laurence presented the physical involvement and the sexuality without the other qualities. His performance was the more acceptable to the majority perhaps because of the times in which we live, but who is to say with certainty which was the nearer to Shakespeare's imagined man? Does not the effect of the finished performance depend greatly on the audience's own needs and desires? Our communication is after all to our own generation, and must be acceptable in terms of current styles and fashions. As Peter Hall, Director of the Royal Shakespeare Company, said in a talk given to his cast:

> . . . we don't know how the Elizabethans spoke Shakespeare. I can tell you to 'speak the speech trippingly on the tongue'. I can observe that they must have played at speed . . . and we can all sense that their tongues were athletic, their minds agile, and the medium immediate and stimulating. But where does this get us? We have to synthesise an experience of the plays to *our* audience. . . .

This is as true of verse speaking as it is of acting, and while being as true to the poet as the actor is to his text, we must reproduce him in terms which will unite him to and not alienate him from his audience.

Thus interpretations of poems, whilst they strive to come as near as possible to the poet's personality, voice, and intention, will vary in a hundred subtle ways according to the tone and temperament and shades of emphasis given in the speaking.

Mention must be made here of the numerous poets who are recording their own poetry for posterity. We may now listen to such widely differing personalities as Dylan Thomas, John Betjeman, Phillip Larkin, T. S. Eliot, and, amongst many others, the highly individual style of Stevie Smith. But are these the voices that we should find from the page? How far does a poet mask his true self when he reads? Has he the capacity for being absolutely honest and true to his innermost being when he sits down in front of a microphone and vocalises his experience? If not, we may well be listening to 'mask' and not 'face'. Or through sheer familiarity with his material, the poet may 'underplay' his own poem; perhaps his very modesty will act as a barrier to full communication.

The poets themselves differ as much as any other body of opinion when it comes to reading poetry aloud. Some, like Yeats and Vernon Watkins, demand meticulous attention to rhythm, not caring, perhaps, that an absolutely fixed rhythm must inevitably, by its sheer monotony, have a soporific effect on all but the most enthusiastic of listeners. T. S. Eliot can sound to some ears so academic and dry that it is hard to pick out the salient points from the general body of the matter. Others tend to have repeated cadences in their voices which give a slightly melancholy dying fall to all their reading which, even if the poem requires this, needs to be varied on the listener's ear. This is not meant to be criticism of the value of the poet reading, but regret that even here the poem's import is sometimes reduced in significance because monotonous sound is intruding itself, much as highly charged sound intrudes itself when some actors read. The poem, after all, is more important even than the poet. However, the poet reading is always trying to be true to his poem, and this absolute integrity is a privilege to listen to, and when allied to the poet's actual presence can be an overwhelming experience and seldom to be forgotten.

Should it then be copied by the student-speaker? Obviously not. There is no place for mimicry in the speaking of poetry. A copy is just a copy and has no life of its own. It lacks spontaneity, humanity, and individuality, and these are essential factors in communication. Besides, we cannot hope to reproduce 'voice' without reproducing 'thought', and we can only find the poet's thought through our own intellectual mechanism. Without this we are merely a speaking machine delivering sound without its appropriate thought, which could as well be delivered by a robot or computer. We must think with the poet, and if we do this, then something of his 'voice' will emerge.

Then words cannot be divorced from meaning – the sense of words cannot be ignored. To refer to Francis Berry once again: he suggests that a student may well be able to reproduce the voice of Milton's 'L'Allegro', while he cannot manage the voice of 'Paradise Lost'. But is not the fact that he cannot produce the voice of 'Paradise Lost' caused by the fact that he cannot produce in his own intellectual thinking the thought of 'Paradise Lost'? Berry goes on to say that perhaps at 50 he may gain a capacity to read 'Paradise Lost', but have lost the ability to reproduce 'L'Allegro'. Anyone who heard Dame Sybil Thorndike playing St. Joan on radio at the age of 84 or Dame Peggy Ashcroft playing Rosalind at the age of 50 knows that this is not necessarily true. The human voice acquires maturity through its maturity of thought, but it does not, if it is well trained and kept in condition, thereby discard the semblance of youth. But, of course, it must be so trained and maintained, as is the dancer's body, and Dame Margot Fonteyn at the age of 47 was better able to produce the semblance of youth, through her superb technique, than the equally talented and actually youthful student. She had not only learned maturity of thinking through experience of life, but she had learned how to be selective in performance and how to suggest the 'youth' which she has never allowed herself to forget. Thus the verse speaker must grow to the mature voice of 'Paradise Lost' while never losing touch with the earlier voice of 'L'Allegro'. It is again a matter of developing technique.

But to all this must be added the fact that the essence of a poem does not depend on the voice in which it is spoken. The essence of the John Clare poem quoted was the deep despairing loneliness of spirit common to all sufferers of mental disorder. This is surely an abstract quality which can be felt by young or old, educated or rustic. It transcends sex, time, class, or creed. Here we must refer yet again to Berry's admirable opening chapter on language in which he says 'In poetry language is agent and not instrument' (these terms need defining; thus 'agent' – one who exerts power or produces an effect; and 'instrument' – thing used in performing an action, person so made use of . . .), and, finally, 'Language to a poet is not a means to an end, it is the end itself – the language in the constitution of a poem *is* the experience. . . .'

Thus, in the true speaking of the 'Frightened Ploughman', language and experience will have become one. The listeners should be left, not with a voice, but with an experience – John Clare's experience. The words are a channel through which, in the speaker's preparation of the poem, he is led back to the original experience. They are the communicating link through which the poet speaks to the reader, and the reader then communicates to his audience. Neither words nor experience exist alone. They are interdependent and cannot be separated. That they will have to be so separated during preparation of the poem is one of the reasons why poems take so long to prepare. No sensitive speaker should be willing to speak a poem until he has managed, through technique and imagination, to re-fuse language and experience into one expression. It is when language is given dominance over experience or experience is allowed to dominate language that failure or partial failure to communicate the poem's essence is the result. The full realization of any poem of merit may take years to acquire and will be constantly developing as the speaker increases technical mastery and imaginative perception. Complete success must always be very rare as in any art form, but the occasional glimpses of realisation show the potential.

In *Words in the Mind* Charles Davy describes a game of chess in which one player was able to project himself into the actual assembly of pieces and direct operations. He became, in his imagination, the 'essence' of the game. This can happen when preparing a poem. One can become, temporarily, the actual experience, the 'self-hypnotising feat of inward concentration', to quote Davy again. This entails a lengthy process of speaking and concentrating, but there is no mistaking it when it happens. It is like entering into an imaginary world which is there, complete, all the time, awaiting one's presence. Sometimes it is merely glimpsed as through a half-open door. Sometimes it disappears altogether. There has to be a brief period of waiting before speaking for the 'world' to assemble, but if the mood, atmosphere, audience, situation, etc., are right, then language and experience become one at that moment and can be communicated as one to the listeners.

> There never was a world for her
> Except the one she sang, and singing made.
> (W. STEVENS, 'The Idea of Order at Key West'.)

Practising poets must be more highly skilled in 'hearing' a poem from the page than are teachers, actors, or readers, many of whom fail to realise that the printed signs on the page are not the poems, and that these have to be sought for. Poets who read constantly in public do find that their 'voices' are modified by the thought of actually vocalising what they have written, and for this reason they may well make linguistic adjustments. It is one thing, for instance, to hear in the mind such evocative words as 'frost-stung' and drift-wood', but if the speech organs of the poet can only manage 'fros-stung' and drif-wood' he may well think again before giving his tongue-tip such gymnastics. On the other hand, the magnificent vocal instrument of Dylan Thomas surely caused him to give himself such lines from 'Fern Hill' to read aloud as:

> Walking warm out of the whinnying green stable
> On to the fields of praise.

There is, also, the poem which shows the poet's desire to communicate through words. From 'The Idea of Order at Key West' by Wallace Stevens, already quoted, we have:

> The maker's rage to order *words* of the sea,
> *Words* of the fragrant portals, dimly starred,
> And of ourselves, and of our origins,
> In ghostlier demarcations, keeneer *sounds*. [*My italics*.]

Or Edward Thomas, from 'Words',

> Choose me, you English words.

In such poems the speaker will feel with the poet the 'incapacity of language', which cannot always be made to serve the poet's full purpose.

This might be a good moment to discuss the vexed question of memorising. If a poem is to be 'entered into' in the way described, it must be memorised – it must literally be 'learned by heart'. It need not be spoken from memory in public. Mere test of memorised words is nothing. But it must at some time have been spoken without recourse to the printed text. The very act of memorising establishes aspects of the poem which may well be overlooked in a reading. It can also be a test of a poem's completeness. There must be no redundant words insufficiently explored by the speaker, no 'emotion slopping about loose'. Sometimes one may begin by feeling that certain phrases are a little superfluous, a mere garnish on the main dish. But this may well be one's own lack. A deeper search will reveal hidden significances, the poem assembling itself like a jigsaw puzzle.

In the writing of a poem poets often say they find a rhythm forcing its way through their consciousness before the words which are to carry that rhythm. This may be a phrase or a complete line which will then determine the rhythm of the whole. Memorising can well be undertaken in a similar way, and the rhythm memorised before the actual words. Thus it becomes possible in rehearsal to keep a line going with inarticulate sound, substituting actual words as they are memorised, and while single phrases or whole lines will immediately spring into the memory, others take a considerable time. Just as some poems seem to 'write themselves' in their entirety, the poet being in a trance-like state, others have to be laboured over. So it is with memorising, and this is better undertaken in whole rather than in part, because in this way the poem grows in its totality and overall shape and climax grow with rhythm and words. In longer poems one or two stanzas can be tackled together, with the poem read in its entirety before being put aside, so that the whole is growing with the part.

As time goes by, the seemingly complete 'world' of the poem may well need modifying in the light of new experience. To come back to a poem after a period of months or years may well demand reassessment. It is to be hoped that a deeper appreciation of the experience contained in the poem will have taken place. Sometimes the reverse can occur and a poem can be found not to have stood the necessary test of time. But it should be remembered that it served its purpose at some point and may well serve for others, and though its truth may now seem simple rather than profound, it may well make its point to students or audiences not yet ready for weightier material.

To summarise: in the early stages a poem may well mirror a comparable personal experience. This will soon lead to interest in the poem's creator, and study of the poet should follow. Just as the poet wishes to be judged from his poetry and not his public personality, so reading the poet's poems will tell us what we need to know about him far more than the majority of biographies, which must always be slanted to the opinions and personalities of the biographers. If letters are available they can be immensely revealing, as, of course, are diaries. The reading of collected poems in chronological order will reveal the developing mind, and some poets give careful consideration to the order in which their poems appear in published form, hoping they will be read in this order wherever possible.

Attempting to find the man behind the words is comparable to the most delicate and subtle characterisation, and is a fascination in itself. But a poem is an end in itself, too, and not a means to an end, and language and experience must eventually fuse into one expression, which can then be communicated to others.

To whom are we to communicate?

CHAPTER 3

The Audience

O what is it that makes me tremble so at voices?
(WALT WHITMAN, 'Vocalism'.)

Listeners to poetry have to make more readjustments than listeners to prose because the matter is more compact and concentrated and the pattern less familiar. Of course, a simple poem is more easily digested than, say, a complicated prose lecture on higher mathematics, but in general the principle is true. Rather as we adjust our balance to walking uphill or in a high wind, so a group of people preparing to listen to poetry need to make aural adjustments and to be encouraged to jettison prejudice and preference.

What sort of mental state do we require of our listeners for the communication of poetry? Roger Fry in his book *Vision and Design* says the audience for any art needs to be in a state of 'disinterested intensity of contemplation', but Susanne Langer argues that such a rarified condition would seriously limit the audience for any art. In *Feeling and Form* she goes on to state that 'Art is the creation of forms symbolic of human feeling'. This seems altogether warmer and more immediate. In the theatre Brecht did his best to dismiss the atmosphere of 'spellbinding' which dramatic presentation may induce, and his influence is still widely felt. Yet with poetry, surely 'spellbound' is just what we need to be as audiences if the language to which we are listening is to penetrate beyond the everyday conversational level.

But the speaker himself must not be spellbound. No teacher, speaker, or reader can ever afford to be so wrapped up in his subject that he forgets for one moment his reason for speaking at all, namely to communicate something to his listeners. Therefore his first concern must always be to

29

them, and he must be sure that he is easily and clearly HEARD. The vowels he speaks will carry the TONE and RESONANCE; the consonants will divide the audible sound and give clarity. The FORWARD PLACING of the voice in the mouth will throw the sound out and aid projection. Control of breath will ensure that phrases are unbroken and that sentences do not fade away at the full stops. Acoustics are frequently inadequate, but voice production classes will help to teach clear articulation and control of tone in over-resonant halls (see Chapter 4).

But no amount of technical know-how and training will replace or obviate the mental desire to communicate. Providing that the voice is well supported by breath, that there is a real desire to be audible to the back row, and that there is concentration on the subject-matter, then something will be communicated.

It is a useful part of any speaker's equipment to be able to imagine himself a member of any audience to whom he is speaking, and to anticipate at least a part of their needs. There is no doubt at all that the necessary 'empathy' between speaker and audience must be created before anything of import can be fully communicated. Therefore opening remarks, introductions to poems, etc., need to be well chosen and delivered with care while the speaker 'feels his way' and attempts to analyse the response he is getting. For actors this could be compared to the exposition of a play.

Alternatively some will advocate the 'shock' tactics of plunging in with reasonably difficult material, to jolt the listeners and gain their full attention. The approach will depend on circumstances and knowledge of the type of audience to whom one is speaking. Here the teacher would seem to have an advantage since he knows, perhaps only too well, the measure of his audience. Indeed, if the right atmosphere exists in the classroom, this can well be a tremendous advantage. On the other hand, the teacher himself is an all too familiar figure to his class, and if his subject is unpopular, this can be a great drawback compared with the novelty value of the visiting poet or lecturer facing the same class. In a theatre the actor-reader has an initial advantage over the teacher in the classroom since neither he nor his subject has been pre-judged and found wanting, or presumably that audience would not be there.

At a public recital the audience have come because they wish to hear poetry and have paid to do so. This must in some measure affect their response, since they will certainly expect their money's worth. Sometimes this response is uninhibited, warm, and informal. Sometimes it can seem withdrawn and inflexible. Usually it consists of a little of each. According to how the speaker judges and meets whatever response he finds, the success or partial success or failure of the reading depends. Therefore audience-sensitivity is essential. It is necessary to be able to gauge the needs and requirements of the majority and to satisfy them. Then this majority will usually sweep the minority along with them.

The main body of the reading or lesson will have been designed and rehearsed and shaped with a particular purpose in view. This will be revealed through the choice and arrangement of material. What must remain flexible is presentation. There must be preparation of the listeners so that they are moulded into the right frame of mind to receive the programme which has been decided upon. It can often be necessary to increase extempore explanations or to reduce these according to the 'feeling' which comes across. As to this 'feeling' – one cannot be more specific. It is an abstract thing which only experience teaches us to judge. It is a lesson which all speakers have to learn, and it is the unknown quantity in any reading wherever it takes place.

Unfortunately it is never possible to know what effect any particular group is going to have on the speaker. Beginners tend to be thrown off their balance if the listeners react in an unexpected way. A poem which has been read aloud in the respectful silence of one's own room can seem a very different thing when presented to a barrage of coughing or fidgeting. These physical manifestations of unease in the listeners are well worth noting, however, especially if they tend to increase. If listeners are really 'held' they will suspend their movements until a break occurs, and they must always be given this break at regular intervals.

But restlessness is not the only distraction the speaker must expect. Sometimes lack of response to humorous material can be most disconcerting. The speaker may feel his courage melting away and he may long to get on to the heavier stuff – or vice versa – feeling that perhaps he has chosen the wrong material. This will have the most disastrous effect, since if he loses confidence in himself, his listeners will not be slow to follow. Sometimes the listeners will respond more than expected, and this, too, can be upsetting. The listening group can appear to be taking over the reading, dictating its terms, and therefore beyond the speaker's control. This can be unnerving at any stage and usually results in the communication taking a downward instead of an upward curve. It is always necessary for the speaker to be in charge. Therefore the too responsive group needs controlling as much as the unresponsive needs stirring.

Experience teaches that the most valuable asset to any speaker is the ability to pause, to wait, to suspend the reading until both listeners and speakers are ready for it to continue. Standing quite still and relaxed in front of an audience or class will have the effect of making them quite still and relaxed also. They will feel the control and respond to it. Unfortunately, inexperienced speakers who get into deep waters tend, like swimmers, to thrash about in small circles at great speed, instead of – to continue the analogy – turning over on their backs and floating.

Experience will make audience hazards fall into certain general categories which can be anticipated and dealt with providing there is flexibility of approach. In public performance the hazards likely to be encountered are poor acoustics, dim or harsh lighting, uncomfortable seating, creaking chairs, cold draughty halls or hot smoke-filled rooms, no facilities for refreshments during an interval, lack of amenities for the speaker, to say nothing of outside distractions. These can include traffic, church bells, chiming clocks, beat groups, washing up, or even (though this can be turned into an asset) bird-song.

Poetry needs silence. In the modern world this is hard to find and hard to create. Yet the reader of poetry must create it, or at least must seem to create it. Oddly enough, if the audience's attention is openly drawn to some of the drawbacks, then they will no longer notice them. Tell an audience not to worry at all if they feel like coughing, and they will immediately feel less need to do so. Apologise for the beat group upstairs and suddenly no one hears it any more. Mention the trains rumbling by at every 10 minutes, and no more trains run. If the room is small and over-

crowded, see that there is time to shuffle and change position; if sparsely
filled, suggest a closing up of ranks, which always increases communication. Consider yourself always as a member of that audience and decide
what you would need. See that you are a member of an audience for
poetry every now and again, not only to learn from others but also to
remind yourself of some of the hazards.

Yet beyond all this the unknown quantity still exists. Sometimes even
in the most ideal circumstances a reading fails to grip, to stimulate, or to
excite. Surprisingly, perfection of venue and décor can sometimes be
chilling to sensitive performers. On the other hand, many speakers will
recall that some of their most memorable moments of communication
came in the least promising circumstances. It is as though the very limitations of the situation fuse speaker and audience into one conspiracy of
shared experience, literally in spite of all the difficulties.

But the fact remains that this should not be. Just as a nation should not
require a war or national disaster to bring out its 'finest hour', a poetry
reading should not be given such difficulties to overcome. An audience
must be considered, respected, even wooed, and this includes decent
seating, lighting, acoustics, visual presentation, and refreshment for body
as well as soul. Listening to poetry requires complete concentration from
both speaker and audience. It is an experience of delicacy and subtlety,
and cannot take place without considerable rapport between reader and
listeners. What circumstances would seem to be ideal?

Leaving aside the classroom for the moment, for a public reading a
small theatre, concert-room, art gallery or lecture hall, with accommoda-
tion for not more than three to four hundred. A slightly raised platform
or tiered seats and good acoustics and lighting so that all may see and hear
without effort. On the platform a solid table with either chairs or stools
and, if possible, lecterns well lit and adjustable. Furniture to be functional
and decorative and of varying heights, and, if possible, again one object of
aesthetic interest only such as flowers, statuary, or coloured drape. The
listener's eye needs to be satisfied but not distracted, so that his ear can
happily take over. Eccentricities of clothes or mannerisms can always be
forgiven the poet, but are rarely acceptable in an actor or reader; so dress

should be becoming to the wearer without being in itself so eye-catching that it rivets attention.

Delivery will be dealt with in succeeding chapters, but this could be the place for some discussion of stance, gesture, movement, and grouping. There are no rules, but in general terms the following guides have found to be acceptable to most audiences.

STANCE

The odd idea has grown up in some quarters that a lyric poem should be delivered from a standing position with the arms to the sides and the eyes focused straight ahead. It is even possible to find this insisted upon by some speech examiners. This unnatural emphasis on a particular position usually has the undesirable effect of drawing attention to the stance rather than to the poem. While it is true that lyric poetry requires little or no assistance in gesture or movement of any kind from the speaker, it is frequently better communicated from a more relaxed position. Sitting down or holding a book in the hands is far more natural and therefore more acceptable to the listener. If hands and arms are not adding to the communication, they are better employed holding a book than hanging loosely at the sides, and the presence of the book does have the effect of removing for all time the slight air of 'recitation'. The poem itself will usually impose on the speaker the best position for communication. Mood and content will dictate this. Reflective poetry seems to come more easily from a sitting position, particularly if this is implied in the actual wording. For instance, in 'Sunday Morning' by Wallace Stevens the woman is sitting in a dressing-gown musing on the subject of life, death, and religion. Therefore to stand to read this poem would seem to work against its content. On the other hand, a strong lyrical ballad like Charles Causley's 'Nursery Rhyme of Innocence and Experience', where the boy is standing on the quay looking out to sea, would seem less natural spoken from a sitting position. 'Summer Farm' by Norman McCaig works very well read from a low stool, since in the poem the poet is lying in the grass and observing the sky, the farm, and a passing grasshopper, and this slight change of position helps to indicate this. Indeed, each new poem would seem to need a very slight change of stance to suggest a new approach, a new atmosphere, or a new poet.

All variations can be worked out with the sole idea of providing variety to the eye as well as to the ear and maintaining the audience's full attention. A speaker, standing quite still for too long in one position, can become mesmeric to an audience, who will then tend to lose the import of what he is saying. If there is more than one reader, then positioning will be worked out between them, so that whoever is reading is in the dominant position – the other keeping quite still and not, as one so often sees, fidgeting with his papers and impatiently awaiting his turn to continue. The other occupants of the platform should give as much attention to the reader of each poem as they hope to get themselves from the audience, or as members of the cast of a play give to each other. Any distracting movement on their part will instantly rivet the audience's attention to them and away from the poem, and concentration is so easily broken.

GESTURE

Use gesture only sparingly and only as a means of emphasis. Poetry is a disciplined and exact art and its words are chosen with accuracy and seldom need underlining in any way. But an elegant movement of the hand and wrist when reading the eighteenth-century satirists can serve to point the period, or a more sweeping movement of the whole arm could emphasis the virility of the Elizabethan era. In dramatic or narrative poetry a slight change of position of the head or angle of the body can indicate different 'characters', and in humorous verse there can be opportunities for some movement and gesture, particularly when reading to younger children. For example, in 'First Fight' by Vernon Scannell a suggestion of the boxer's defensive movement can underline the dramatic quality of the poem's atmosphere, and 'Hide and Seek' by Eleanor Farjeon is more fun for the listeners if they can 'see' the various hiding-places which the children find in their game. But all movement must be carefully and economically planned with as much care as is given to delivery.

FACIAL EXPRESSION

Facial expression is also a means of emphasis. It must be a reflection of thought only and never superimposed. Thus if the thought is right and the facial muscles flexible, the face will emphasise the words being spoken. Faces can sometimes convey meanings more than voices, and while this may be an asset in live performance, it is no help when broadcasting or recording, since here gesture and facial expression must be implied through voice alone. To some extent facial expression must modify vocal delivery, e.g. it is difficult to sound joyous with a dead-pan face or mournful with a broad grin, but a speaker needs to be sure that his voice is expressing the poem and not only his face. Some superb B.B.C. readers are much less interesting in live performance, and some magnetic actors are greatly reduced on record or in a broadcast. Here the sparing use of tape-recorder can be invaluable and salutary, to check that communication is not relying too much on physical presence.

MOVEMENT AND GROUPING

It is seldom wise to move about during a poem as the fine thread of communication is so easily broken. But again there are exceptions. For example, Browning's 'My Last Duchess' is immensely effective if accompanied by a slow walk through the gallery by the Duke, who then sits to admire the portrait of his late wife. Similarly, passages from Byron's 'Don Juan' or 'Beppo' can gain from quite broad gesture and movement, and D. H. Lawrence's 'Bat' certainly needs the head movement and change of eye focus, as does his 'Mosquito'. Perhaps a general rule could be that movement and gesture must always be subordinate to words and used only to enhance or emphasise, never being allowed to distract. This applies to solo readers, small groups, or choirs.

On the subject of choirs and choral speech, grouping and movement can be immensely helpful to mood and atmosphere. But this is a specialised study, and the reader is directed once again to the bibliography for expert help and advice.

Before leaving this field of poetry recital for the teacher reading in classroom, there is just this to be said. An audience entering a small theatre, as opposed to a lecture hall, concert room, or art gallery, is conditioned to expect a slightly more theatrical approach. Therefore some consideration of this need should govern choice of material and presentation.

The use of music, selected and played with due regard for the overall shape and intention of the programme, is an excellent aid. String and wind instruments seem to compliment the human voice to perfection, though the piano can also be a most discreet partner to poetry. If music is used to underline or round off a poem, then ideally it should be original work and not known in any other context. The difficulty here is that the music itself may be musically inferior to the poem it is complementing, and musical enthusiasts in the audience may find this distressing. But if, like gesture, stance and movement, the music is simply there to enhance the poem, and no more is expected of it as music, then it will serve to sustain or create a mood which is implicit in the poem, and allow one poem to be savoured while the next is prepared for.

If the musician is a solo artist and not accompanist, then groups of poems will be followed by a similar length of music and this can give a pleasing balance for the audience's pleasure. Poetry and song recitals can be exceptionally rewarding for the listeners, and the occasional speaking of a poem followed by a musical setting of the same poem, or vice versa, can be a further variation to delight both ear and mind (see Chapter 8, Preparation of Programmes). Recorded music with live voice never seems very satisfactory, though in some cases it may be all that is possible if no musicians are available.

Finally, the marriage of poetry and jazz has opened up exciting new avenues of experience for audiences able to accept a new and challenging medium. Here the improvised nature of jazz provides a marvellous contrast to the more disciplined nature of poetry. The telling effect of simple words spoken to music written especially for them, but still in the jazz idiom, can give to both words and music a significance beyond that which either could have achieved alone. It is as though both the jazz poem and the accompanying music are lacking a dimension which their coming together then creates.

Every generation needs something new to enthuse over. It may well be that poetry and jazz supply this. At its best it can have the simplicity of folk song without the banality and repetitious words and the excitement of 'pop' without the sterility of lyric and tune. In fact it can provide young people with the emotional stimulus and intellectual satisfaction referred to in Chapter 1, and it does have the effect of removing from poetry the too academic approach and association (see Chapter 7).

Which brings us to the most important audience of all, namely the audience in the classroom. Most important since, if properly approached, they could form the recital audiences of the future. The main difficulties for the class must be over-familiarity with surroundings and reader, physical discomfort, atmosphere of 'lesson' rather than recreation. All these must surely work against successful communication of complex emotional matter. The wonder is that English teachers manage such a high proportion of success given such unsatisfactory conditions. Undoubtedly there are many administrative difficulties in moving whole classes from one room to another. But for science they go to the laboratory, for music or P.E. to the hall or gym; for art they go to the art room. Could they not go the library for poetry? Could not seating be more informal? Atmosphere relaxed and geared to enjoyment? Free exchange of ideas and of readers? School magazines stimulate and encourage the writing of poetry. Why not readings of these poems arranged and given for other classes, or for parents? Combining with the other arts subjects is obvious. Music, drama, and modern dance are frequently linked in imaginative presentation, and the use of both choral and solo verse speaking could be a natural part of these activities. In some schools, of course, this is already done, but no one would pretend that such schools are in the majority.

It would be presumptuous to offer suggestions to teachers on how to handle discussion of poems after they have been read, but there is just this to be said. If, as we have seen, listeners take a little time to adjust to poetry in the middle of a busy day, then reading several poems without a break does give time for this adjustment to take place. The poems can be linked by poet, or period or content, or present differing aspects of a chosen theme. It is then the total poems which will be considered rather than particular aspects of any one, remembering Susanne Langer's warning in *Feeling and Form* that 'the import of a poem is lost in a prose paraphrase'. Also it seems only fair to allow the poet the last word after discussion and to hear the poems read again before the class ends. Ideally this should be undertaken by the class themselves to avoid any fixed interpretation being presented, however unconsciously, by the teacher.

To summarise: audience sensitivity is essential whether in theatre, lecture hall, or classroom. The speaker must always be in control but must be flexible in presentation to meet whatever hazards may appear. All presentation to be subordinate to the poem's needs and the audience's enjoyment. The teacher or reader must possess the technical equipment to give more than just a straight 'reading' which is sufficient only for the most simple of poems. The difference between 'reading' and what we may call 'inhabiting' a poem is very subtle (see following chapter). Listeners may well be unaware of the difference until one poem suddenly appears to spring to life, as can happen when the poet himself reads. If no associated meanings and developments are evoked by the reader, then the symbolic nature of the poem is lost. These developments and meanings should not depend on copious footnotes or pre-knowledge, but should be implicit in the reading. The reading should therefore be what Susanne Langer called 'emotionally transparent'. (This book, *Feeling and Form*, already referred to, is so extensive that it is to be hoped that the few quotations included will serve to lead readers to the source.) If the reader of the poem is only concerned with words and has not found associated meanings, then the audience or class may be interested but will not be moved sufficiently to retain any lasting impression of the poem.

Tolstoy, in *What is Art?*, says:

> To evoke in oneself a sensation which one has experienced before, and having evoked it in oneself, to communicate this sensation in such a way that others may experience the same sensation . . . so that other men are infected by these sensations and pass through them; in this does the activity of art consist.

CHAPTER 4

Preparation of the Instrument

Part I

> Are you full-lung'd and limber-lipp'd from long trail?
> From vigorous practise? from physique?
> Do you move in these broad lands as broad as they?
> Come duly to the divine power to speak words?
>
> (WALT WHITMAN, 'Vocalism'.)

The difference between 'reading' a poem and 'inhabiting' a poem is very subtle. It is perhaps best explained by an example. To take some words known to all, words which have been sung, spoken, declaimed, intoned, muttered, murmured, and mumbled by most of the inhabitants of the western hemisphere at some time or another, may prove the point; namely the Lord's Prayer:

> Our Father, which art in Heaven, Hallowed be Thy Name. Thy Kingdom come. Thy will be done, in earth as it is in Heaven. Give us this day our daily bread. And forgive us our trespasses. As we forgive them that trespass against us. And lead us not into temptation; but deliver us from evil. . . .

How many people saying those words ever give any thought to their associated meanings? For instance, 'Our Father'. What does that conjure up? To children perhaps an old man with a long white beard sitting up in Heaven on a golden throne. To adults perhaps a benevolent spirit who created the earth, or an intellectual concept of an indefinable nature. And 'which art in Heaven'—what does 'Heaven' suggest? A perfect version of the earth? Something up in the skies – over the rainbow? Or, as Wallace Stevens suggests in 'Sunday Morning',

> neither the golden underground
> Nor isle melodious where spirits gat them home,
> Nor visionary south nor cloudy palm remote on Heaven's hill.

40

'Hallowed be Thy Name', the prayer continues. The dictionary meaning of hallowed says: 'Make holy, honour as holy'. What are we thinking when we say 'Hallowed be Thy Name'? What actual thought is in our minds? And then 'Thy Kingdom come'. Do we ever stop to think what that would mean? Can we possibly contemplate it since we do not know what God's Kingdom is? Or are we hoping that one day God will rule all and that His will will be done on earth as it is in Heaven?

Many people have rejected set prayers because it is so difficult to keep the mind on something which has become meaningless through repetition, and which must be rooted in faith and not intellect. Certainly we should never allow ourselves to say words without thought. If we believe in this prayer, then we must think out each phrase and be sure that when we say 'Our Father, which art in Heaven', etc., we are really addressing a deity and hoping that He will one day sort out all the troubles of the earth, see that we have sufficient to eat, and overlook our failings. We must think this every time we say those words, and through this practice we may get a revelation of what the words are all about. To begin with, we shall need to say the words more slowly while we ensure that only the right thoughts are in our minds and no others. But gradually we should be able to speak the prayer at its own rhythmic pace and still so order our minds that word and thought are one.

This is what we have to do in order to 'inhabit' a poem. We have to so order our minds that words and thoughts are one. As with the prayer, it is only too easy to speak words quite intelligently and intelligibly while thinking only partly of the words we are using. The mind is not fully engaged. But this has only superficial value to either speaker or listener. The value comes when we have trained our minds to think and our voices to express at one and the same time. Speaking poetry allows us to borrow the poet's thoughts, and thus extends and develops our own powers both of thinking and of speaking.

To take other examples. 'Shall I compare thee to a summer's day?', says Shakespeare (Sonnet No. XVIII). Would we ever have had that particular thought about an object of our desire and affection? 'When I consider how my light is spent / 'Ere half my days in this dark world and wide', said

Milton ('On his Blindness'). The speaker must be able to embrace the hideousness of approaching blindness with all its implications for a writer of that time. The audacity of John Donne addressing Death in person with 'Death be not proud, though some have called thee / Mighty and dreadful . . .' and Browning's 'I wonder, do you feel as I' from the opening of 'Two in the Campagna'. Those last few words sum up the whole desire of human beings to know what is in another's mind. We cannot just read the words; we have to think them and feel them and suffer them as the poet did, and then discipline the thought, the feeling, and the suffering into an art form which will illuminate the experience for the listeners.

Can this really be done in just a 'reading'; or by a completely untrained speaker? Is it only a talented few who can attempt this difficult task? Or is it possible that those with a love for and understanding of poetry in all its forms can certainly improve their reading out of all knowledge once they have appreciated what is required? To reach the sort of standard achieved by Sir John Gielgud in his recent recording of Shakespeare's sonnets is something quite beyond contemplation for most of us, but teachers with their literary knowledge and understanding, and actors with an already trained instrument, can certainly give enormous satisfaction to both classes and audiences.

Training the mind is difficult. Teaching ourselves to cast out all extraneous matter while we are speaking the poet's words needs considerable practice. But it is a practice which will enrich the whole personality and individuality of the student and will open up a new world for those who are not too busy to persevere and stay the course. To quote from the foreword to *Zen in the Art of Archery*,

> If one really wishes to be master of an art, technical knowledge of it is not enough. One has to transcend technique so that the art becomes an 'artless art' growing out of the Unconscious.

The following suggestions for training are only the result of one person's experiments. They must be adapted to suit individual needs. But they have been tested and in some small degree found to work, or this book would not have been commissioned. If they prove a starting point for one person with more talent, more intellect, and more energy, then they will have been worth while.

Discussion of preparation must take into consideration the fact that all possess a built-in instrument, and therefore have already acquired some part of the necessary techniques in their everyday communication. It is at once the strength and the weakness of this art form. The strength in the fact that all can attempt, but the weakness in that many may do so for the wrong reasons, i.e. to demonstrate not the poet's skill but their own. As Susanne Langer says:

> We do not want the subjective interpretation that makes art a vehicle for the performer's personal anxieties and moods, but the element of ardor for the import conveyed.

In no art is the intrusion of self more likely than in the spoken arts, since these are nearest to personal communication through the medium of speech; therefore the need for some training aimed at the removal of self.

On the other hand, it is true that a student will make a far better job of reading a poem without any training at all than, say, any comparable student of the violin. It is possible to hear excellent first readings from quite untrained speakers, and frequently more acceptable than half-trained elocutionists. Hence perhaps the feeling that there is no training which is really helpful. But the fact is that teachers may have to read the same poem many times, as will the professional performer, and the trained speaker will aim to produce the initial spontaneity at any time and in any circumstances.

Some audiences seem quite content with sound alone. Yet the sound of words divorced from their meaning cannot really stand comparison with the sound of music, whereas the sound of words made significant by meaning can particularise and penetrate in a way no other art can match.

If the training demands seem rigorous, consider the young singer who spends the first year of training doing nothing but breathing exercises and never sings a note, or the student of dance who every single day of his artistic life must perform the same monotonous exercises at the bar, or the musician with his endless scales. Surely this humility could be matched by students of verse speaking.

To return to the musician. In his foreword to *Light on Yoga* by B. K. S. Iyengar, Yehudi Menuhin says:

> Reduced to our own body, our first instrument, we learn to play it, drawing from it maximum resonance and harmony. With unflagging patience we refine and animate every cell as we return daily to the attack, unlocking and liberating capacities otherwise condemned to frustration and death.

The study of Yoga is an end in itself and not a means to an end, and to study it properly is a life's work. Many have neither opportunity nor capacity for such dedication, but for those who have it is invaluable. For others a study of basic mime can teach relaxation, control, flexibility, and sensitivity. Mime forms the basis of training for the actor, based on the work of such outstanding teachers as Irene Mawer, whose book *The Art of Mime* is a standard work on the subject. Mime must not be confused with improvisation, free drama, or even the speech gesture used in ballet. It is, to use the words of Irene Mawer, 'The use of the body as a means of expression of thought, emotion and character'.

The general aim in the teaching of mime is 'To develop personalities in whom mind and body are perfectly co-ordinated and controlled to become an instrument of expression'.

The training involves each part of the body in turn, its significance as an expressive instrument, and the means of developing its power by physical and dramatic exercise. No one part is developed at the expense of any other, and the whole is mind directed. The training aims at developing muscular control, nervous sensitivity, rhythm, flexibility, and strength, the entire body forming an expressive whole.

What is so often overlooked or misunderstood is that all mime is based on WORDS. Every gesture of occupational movement takes its rhythm and timing from the words which would describe it and are spoken in the mind, though not with the voice. Thus 'I pick up this potato and place it in this bowl of water. Then I take a knife and peel off the skin – so.' Or more dramatically: 'I can smell burning. Where can it be coming from? Oh! look – there is a flame under the door!' In training, speech is sometimes used, sometimes not, but the words are always being spoken in the mind. If music is used, then speech phrases match the musical phrases exactly, and it is this discipline which gives delight and reality to good mime work because all actions are based on truth to thought, to word, to action, to music. Removal of the control of word basis into the 'freer' type of improvised drama has tended to weaken the beneficial effects of the exercise, since movement and words have become separated, and once separated self-consciousness is created when the attempt is made to bring them together again. Mime was mistakenly thought to be a too disciplined training for any but specialists, but this was perhaps the deficiency of the teachers rather than of the method, since properly presented it can appeal to all ages and all levels of intelligence. Already it is being realised that to release emotions without then providing a framework of control, can lead to chaotic results which are anything but beneficial.

Thus mime because it uses words . . . is the perfect training for both actor and verse speaker, though as an art form in itself it takes years of dedicated study and results in the skilled artistry of the great French mime Marcel Marceau, for example.

Good teachers of mime are rare outside drama academies, and many potential verse speakers will have neither time for nor the opportunity of studying it. However, much can be achieved along far simpler lines once the necessity for some kind of training has been acknowledged, and though this training may have to be somewhat piecemeal, it will be discussed here as though an ideal foundation were possible. Many students will already have acquired a considerable amount of this training from other fields, though there may be something of value here to help in their further development. There is always more to be learned about any craft, and the following is intended as a spur to enthusiasm and not in any way as a deterent. Art demands discipline, and each speaker will find his own way according to his need. The following are some suggested starting points.

We can approach spoken language from two main aspects:

1. Sense dictating sound – mind leading voice.

2. Sound dictating sense – because the voice is speaking certain words, related thought will be induced.

Advantage of No. 1. The mind is leading and therefore modulating the voice to the appropriate degree for communication of sense, *if the voice is flexible enough to respond.*

Disadvantages of No. 1. In highly charged emotional passages, there can be a danger of too much active thought being projected at the expense of feeling.

Advantage of No. 2. The voice is leading and modulating the thought, i.e. the poet's words, which are his medium, are leading the speaker back to the thoughts which gave rise to those words.

Disadvantages of No. 2. The words may assume a vocal importance of their own which is unsupported by their sense.

To elaborate. Speaking words aloud may often suggest the inner mood and meaning which silent reading of the text failed to do. This is sound dictating sense. In the highly charged emotional passages already referred to, this may well be necessary because the words come as a result of direct feeling, not of considered thought. But silent reading to establish what lies behind the words before vocalising them can also give the meaning which will then modulate the delivery. This is sense dictating sound.

Whichever approach is made the two will eventually become one. Many theatre directors will advocate the sound before sense method when dealing with actors unaccustomed to speaking blank verse, particularly with such a master poet-dramatist as Shakespeare. Shakespeare gives all, and the actor may well succeed best if he surrenders all to the poet and allows himself to be worked upon in this way, in the early stages. Similarly, to speak a poem over and over, allowing its rhythm and 'inner life' to be revealed, is an excellent method of 'finding' the poem behind the words. But once the initial surrender has been made, it is then necessary to establish the thought behind the words and to discipline the mind actually to think the requisite thoughts every time the poem is spoken or the part is played. Many actors will write themselves a second text composed of thoughts, and will then virtually memorise thoughts as well as words. This can also apply to the study of a poem if the complexity of the matter demands this. For complete spontaneity the thought should occur a fraction of a second before the words are spoken, whether in a poem or in the nearest equivalent in drama, the soliloquy, where thoughts are being spoken aloud.* For instance, it is necessary to think 'Is this a dagger that I see before me . . .' before saying it. The mind registers that the eyes are 'seeing' a dagger, and then the words come disciplined in inflection by the thought.

In the poetic/prose plays of Tchekov the thoughts of the characters are frequently of far greater importance than the words they are saying. Consider only the scene between Varia and Lopahin, for example, in Act IV of *The Cherry Orchard*, when laconic banal conversation masks great depths of feeling which literally cannot be uttered. This is the 'indirect dialogue' which the playwright Arthur Adamov thought he had invented for *L'Invasion* and later discovered in Tchekov, but whereas in Tchekov deep feelings are hidden behind meaningless politeness, in Adamov absurd ideas are proclaimed as eternal truths. Many of Ibsen's great characters speak 'lies' for much of the time, and we are made aware that they are 'lies' because the actors speaking them are thinking 'truth' while speaking 'lie'. In the plays of Samuel Beckett and Harold Pinter the silences, during which the actor conveys thought, are frequently of more significance than the dialogue. The plain fact is that thoughts and feelings are more vividly communicated than words, whether the words be memorised, rehearsed, or spontaneous, which is why it is so essential that the thought is right. Then if thoughts and words are in harmony, as in a soliloquy, lyric poem, or sonnet, a very powerful effect is created.

Amateur performers so often convey only their own inner turmoil and self-consciousness, no matter what words they are using, because they have not learned to discipline their thoughts. Political speakers fail often because

---

* A soliloquy can be compared to a lyric poem because it is spoken thought, subjective not objective. Here the arts of the actor and verse speaker are similar, whereas in dialogue the speaking is conditioned by its being reaction to others, and the actor here has a responsibility to his fellow actors as well as to his text.

they appear more concerned to project their personal image than to setting the country to rights. The mental and vocal aim is divided and its effect therefore weakened. There is no mystique or magic about this. The art of speaking, like any other art, is a matter of hard work based on strong, dependable technique. Any speaker who loses concentration on his sub-ject also loses the attention of his audience. His mind is elsewhere. Theirs will be also. This is a further reason for mime training. It helps to teach this concentration and, without any spoken words at all, teaches mind and body to convey volumes of meaning.

Thus while training the body and voice to be responsive, flexible, and varied, we must train the mind to dominate and lead. All exercises should be kept quite separate from expressive work and it is never justified to use any line of any poem or play for any purpose other than the purpose of the dramatist or poet. This may seem obvious, but it is still possible to find teachers who allow poems to be used for training dramatic movement, voice production, improvisation, and even for the strengthening of weak vowel or consonant sounds.

On the subject of mind dominance there is this to be said. Public per-formers may be extroverts, but they are also sensitive people, and without mental discipline it is all too fatally easy to rely on alcohol or drugs to provide the required stimulant and/or tranquilliser which enables some of the worst agonies of apprehension before public performance to be borne. That the necessity gradually increases and the efficaciousness of the remedy soon weakens is too well known to need underlining here. But what should be stressed is that mind training, which could replace this need, is not an impossible and unreachable ideal. Once the idea and the necessity have been firmly planted in the student's mind, they can then be allowed to grow.

But what needs eradicating is the fallacious idea common among some art and drama students that they are in some way above and beyond the need for discipline and hard work. No music or ballet student could make this mistake, perhaps because their training is more exact and standardised. Also because professional opportunities do not come to them without firmly based technical training, whereas it is quite possible for brilliant art or drama students to be launched too soon into responsible work for which they are perhaps ill prepared.

On the other hand, maturity and experience of life are all to the advantage of the painter, actor, or verse speaker. Therapeutically certainly, and sometimes professionally, excellent work can result from 'students' who are well over even official retirement age. By this time they will have found their individual means of expression and the necessary techniques will be absorbed as required. Technique is, after all, a liberator and not an inhibitor, and any student of whatever age who fancies he does not need this framework is seriously limiting his chances of lasting success. The 'rules' are few and must be known before they can, as they often must, be broken. They are the scaffolding upon which to build.

How can we start without the possibility of full-time professional training?

Part II

RELAXATION

All training, whether privately or in a class, should begin with relaxation. There are many books on the subject but nothing will replace the live teacher. Most P.E. and keep-fit classes will give a start and ensure that there is no harm to the physique. After that much can be achieved alone. For instance, daily practice of the stage fall, which is a gradual relaxing of all muscles, can be of great value, providing that the mind at the same time is concentrating on the job of relaxing and gradually working to prevent any extraneous matter from intruding. That extraneous matters will intrude in the early stages is obvious, but with practice the mind can gradually be brought to concentrate only on the business of relaxing, and be empty of all other thoughts. This will take time, but will be eminently worth while. A reputable drama or improvisation class should be able to give basic instruction in the actual fall. Relaxing to the floor, allied to deep breathing, can be beneficial to health as well as to performance and, when linked with mental relaxation, can be an essential first step in mind dominance. It is perhaps worth remembering that Freud said: 'In only a single field of our civilisation has the omnipotence of thoughts been retained, and that is in the field of art.'

In the stage fall it is the weight of the head which pulls the body downwards towards the ground, so the head is leading still, though now in a physical sense. Beginners will be reluctant to relinquish control of the head, rather as in the early stages of swimming, when the swimmer will be reluctant to immerse the head sufficiently to keep the body afloat. But once this point has been established and the thought is directed towards the ground as the desirable position, the actual relaxing of the rest of the muscles of the body becomes easier. The process can be likened to a reconstructed skeleton where the bones are held together by cord. Release the cord and the whole structure collapses. Think of the bones as melting into muscles, all angles become curves; there are many analogies. It must be emphasised that the stage fall needs help from an expert in the early stages, but once first principles have been established, continual daily practice can be done alone. The stages of the fall can be achieved gradually, but they must be rhythmic, and they can be accompanied by suitable music if this is found helpful. Thus:

Breathe in – Breathe out, relaxing head only.
Breathe in – Breathe out, relaxing head and neck.
Breathe in – Breathe out, relaxing head, neck, shoulders, arms and hands.
Breathe in – Breathe out, relaxing down to waist.

Gradually reduce to a crouch, to one knee, to one thigh, to full length on the ground. The fall should be directed to each side alternately, and then should finish with a complete fall and a few minutes of rest and relaxation of mind. When the fall is accomplished correctly, there is no awareness of body other than a gentle sinking sensation.

During all the foregoing the mind should have been thinking only of each part of the anatomy in turn and concentrating on surrendering control each time the body descends and regaining control each time the body ascends. Similarly, the lungs are breathing out when going down, and breathing in when coming up, so the whole process is rhythmical.

Finally, the mind will surrender momentarily to complete the exercise. No mind can be completely empty of thought, and experts on relaxation frequently suggest a colour or a restful scene to assist relaxation of the mind and of the important facial muscles (see *Teaching Mime* by Rose Bruford). Some may find it helpful to imagine the perpendicular shape of the body relaxing into the horizontal, perhaps as a shadow on the wall.

Whatever method is adopted, it will fail time and time again. It is immensely difficult to eradicate from the mind intrusive and irrelevant thoughts. But one day, for perhaps a few seconds, one succeeds, and then there is awareness of what complete concentration really means. But the triumph will not be lasting because the very consciousness of it will once again intrude on the concentration. Thus it is an exercise which continually inspires real endeavour, and it is noticeable that within the partially relaxed state many useful thoughts sometimes arrive, since this state allows ideas to flow.*

A good point to remember is that, as the physical side becomes easier to manage, it becomes correspondingly more difficult to keep the mind fully engaged. Thus all exercises of this nature may start as difficult physically but end as difficult mentally, which is excellent. Drama students, who are frequently 'expert' relaxers, should bear this in mind.

Now obviously the ability to fall to the floor in a relaxed state is in itself of little use to the verse speaker, as there are few poems which call for quite such a dramatic finale. But it is an exercise in mental control as well as in physical relaxation, and it is *controlled relaxation* that we are aiming at. A stage fall will be a painful business unless the muscles are truly relaxed, and this is a great spur to concentration. From the prone position, it is then possible to practise walking, sitting, and standing in an equally relaxed condition. During a performance it is often necessary to check on the tension which will, inevitably, creep in. This tension is responsible for the shaking hands and/or knees, the drying of the throat, lack of control of voice, and, most important of all, lack of ability to concentrate on the matter to be spoken. Now no audience or class requires its

* This sort of progress towards perfection is described with marvellous detail in *Zen in the Art of Archery* by Eugen Herrigel.

speakers or teachers to be superhuman, and often it is heart-warming to realise that the performer is not too sure, too bland, too at ease. But if the initial nervousness which attends any speaker cannot be overcome once the performance or class starts, then the physical manifestations of those nerves will intrude, and full communication will be impossible. The class or audience will not be the only ones to be distracted. The speaker, too, will be distracted, and this can build up until communication between them becomes impossible. This sort of training in control should aid the teacher of a restless class as much as the actor or reader with an indifferent audience.

Perhaps we may now refer to this relaxed state as the neutral position to which the speaker will return after each poem, and upon which he will build each new poem he reads. If, as is likely, he is speaking extempore between the actual poems, then he will speak from this 'neutral' position and build whatever atmosphere and emotional or intellectual state he needs for each poem as he approaches it. It is as well to stress that this so-called 'neutral' position is not his natural state. It is a self-induced state of controlled relaxation. Therefore throughout the reading or class he will always be in control, even if waiting for others to read, waiting for musical interludes, or for discussion or questions, and only when the last word has actually been spoken will he then relinquish his control. Then it is quite possible to find present the shaking hands, etc., which the controlled state had prevented, and it accounts for the exhaustion which is frequently felt after a long reading. The opera singer Tito Gobbi maintains that it is more exhausting to sing one concert of Lieder than to perform three major operas, the concentration being so great. The ability to sustain a programme must be built gradually, and only daily practice will make this possible without strain (see Chapter 8, Preparation of Programmes).

As we progress we must constantly guard against too much facility, fluency, and spurious ease of manner. These can be as much a barrier to communication as hesitancy and tension. We have to be sure that what we convey is the matter in hand, and not either our own self-satisfaction or even, though this is more acceptable, our own humility. The aim is removal of self and complete concentration on the matter to be communicated. The two things go together. If one is completely concentrating on the matter, there is no room for consideration of self. This may sound obvious, but consider how many public speakers, voters of thanks, lecturers, politicians, teachers, actors, and verse speakers leave far more impression of themselves than of their subject. Barriers of personality, accent, manner or mannerisms, appearance, situation, gesture, clothes, or prejudice for the subject (whatever it is) there may well be. But if the subject is made the first priority and presented with vitality, enthusiasm, and humility, these initial barriers will be overcome.

Within the overall 100 per cent concentration, mention must be made of the small corner of the mind which acts as a guide to all who 'perform' in this way, i.e. communicating words to listeners; the standing aside and observing which enables the necessary adjustments to be made, and gives scope for variety of delivery according to the needs of the moment. This is the audience sensitivity referred to in the preceding chapter.

Thus we start by learning to relax the body through mental direction and continue by learning to so discipline the mind that it can cast out all extraneous matter, retaining only the '5 per cent' awareness of audience reaction which must modify presentation and delivery.

THE VOICE

While the body is relaxed is the ideal time to attempt voice exercises which, if properly undertaken, will become mind exercises too, since now the mind will be asked to concentrate on sound only. This will also encourage more perceptive listening. The old axiom that if you listen to yourself no one else will is undoubtedly true, but voice exercises will be useless unless utter concentration at this point is on sound. Here a very sparing use of a tape recorder is invaluable and salutary. We do not hear ourselves as others hear us, and restricted pitch and monotonous cadence or over-inflected speech tunes can spoil our communication if not acknowledged and corrected. We are not training ourselves to have 'beautiful' voices. In any case, who can define a 'beautiful' voice? If by that is meant a voice which produces beautiful sounds, then a too beautiful voice will draw attention to itself rather than to its subject, and this will be a serious handicap. But the voice must be flexible and wide ranged or it will be monotonous, and no amount of concentrated and sincere thinking will avail. If poetry is to be true to life when we speak it, then it will be harsh and ugly at times, as well as warm and mellow, and we will need all the shades of 'colour' that we can find.

All singing exercises can be helpful, provided again that sufficient is known about how the voice should be produced, otherwise harm may be caused to the vocal cords. It is not the function of this book to discuss voice production, but to advocate some lessons with a reputable teacher and then daily practice. As with the stage fall, we need basic principles to guide our first steps and then continued efforts to obtain control over pitch and tone of the voice. It is an established fact that some previously thought tone-deaf students have been helped to sing in tune through mental concentration and developing power to retain a note in the mind, and then to reproduce it. Tone-deaf children are seldom encouraged to sing, so they rarely have a chance to discover their own potential. But a strong mental desire to reproduce a note will go a long way towards creating the ability to do so, and this concentration is excellent mental and aural training, no matter what the age of the student. It is also a first step in vocal liberation, much more difficult to achieve than physical liberation. The ability to sing in tune is no part of the verse speaker's art: it is merely one more step in vocal control. Indeed, an attractive singing voice can be a handicap to some verse speakers, particularly in poetry and jazz (see Chapter 7), since the temptation to sustain a word beyond its spoken length can be great. Opera singers have the same difficulty with spoken dialogue, and it is a measure of their immense skill and control that they can differentiate.

But to extend the range of the singing voice and then to attempt to speak on the varying notes will increase spoken range rapidly and considerably, and can be a fascinating study in itself, provided always that it is used in the right way: not in order to admire one's own splendid sounds, but as a further development in mental control and ability to pinpoint concentration for a given period. From single notes well produced and accurate, develop to arpeggios, maintaining accuracy and control, but getting the voice moving from note to note, as it must eventually in speech. Proceed from sung notes, using all the long vowel sounds, *oo*, *oh*, *aw*, *ah*, *ay*, *ee*. Sing all the long vowels on a scale, speaking the vowels after on a comparable scale. Include the nasal consonant *m* to develop the resonance necessary for good tone, thus: *moo, moh, maw, mah, may, mee*. Now the note will resound in the head cavities, as any good book on voice production will explain. Then add the nasal consonant at the end thus: *moom, mohm, mawm, mahm, maym, meem*.

This same exercise can be used for consonant practice, using the explosives *p* and *b* for lip strength, and the fricatives *t* and *d* for tongue-tip strength, first at the beginning and then at the beginning and end, thus:

poo	*poop*		*too*	*toot*
poh	*pohp*		*toh*	*toht*
paw	*pawp*	and	*taw*	*tawt*
pah	*pahp*		*tah*	*taht*
pay	*payp*		*tay*	*tayt*
pee	*peep*		*tee*	*teet*

(Use the same exercise with *k* and *g* for the soft palate.) If the number of sounds made on one breath can be increased gradually, this also becomes an exercise for BREATH CONTROL.

The long vowel sounds are also excellent practice for easy change of PITCH (very necessary in dramatic or narrative verse). Take the vowel sound *oo*. Speak it on the lowest note you can manage, then on a medium note, then on a high note. Reverse the process. (Watch that the voice moves and not just the head.) Now add varieties of VOLUME, i.e. speak the low note softly, the middle note conversationally, the high note loudly. Reverse this. Try projecting the low note as though to someone far off. Speak the middle note to someone standing close. Speak it harshly, warmly, softly, loudly. Add a mood. In other words, 'colour' the sound by the thought behind it – TONE COLOURING. Use all vocal exercises as though directed to someone else. Attempt to communicate emotion and feeling through a single vowel sound, much as jazz singers do so successfully. After all, it has been said that the only 'pure' sounds we make are groans, sighs, laughs, sobs, etc.

We are thus practising control of PITCH, VOLUME, INFLECTION, TONE-COLOUR, PROJECTION, COMMUNICATION OF EMOTION, CONSONANTS, VOWELS, and BREATH CONTROL, all in one simple exercise and all based on mental direction. If all the long vowels are used in turn, the exercise has great potential variety. But, as with the relaxation tests, the greater the ease of vocal technique the more necessary the need for mental control becomes. It is when technical difficulties are first overcome that many students become over-confident and concentrate less, rather like learner-drivers with their first full licence. They should realise that little can be expressed until basic techniques are safely acquired. Now we can begin to develop.

Finally it is essential to be aware of the wonder of being able to make sound at all. To remind oneself from time to time of the moment of terror when speech is taken away, the total inability to express ecstasy or the emptiness of deep grief. To have a little more respect for sound itself. To think how glibly we all use words and with what inaccuracy, and to enjoy to the full the actual feel of superbly chosen words which it should be a joy to communicate. This sense of wonder, which D. H. Lawrence called our sixth sense, can irradiate all exercises as it should all perfor-mances and can act as a spur to increased effort.

POETIC IMAGERY

Poetry is very much an art of images.* The imagination of the speaker must be as fresh and inventive as that of the poet, though here again the process is reversed. With the poet, the idea or the mood gives rise to the imagery expressed in the words. With the speaker the words provide the imagery, which in turn leads back to the mood or idea. Thus a word or a phrase conjures up a picture in the imagination which must then be com-

* See I. A. Richards, *Principles of Literary Criticism*, Chapter VI (Routledge & Kegan Paul).

municated to the audience. Flexibility here can be achieved through the simple exercise of taking once again the long vowels *oo, oh, aw, ah, ay, ee*, then going swiftly through the alphabet in the mind and adding a consonant where it makes a word, thus.

Taking the vowel sound of *oh*, we get:

bow	*go*	*mow*	*sew*
dough	*hoe*	*no*	*toe*
foe	*low*	*row*	*woe*

The point of the exercise is for quick thinking and what we may call 'instant imagery'. As soon as the word is formed and as it is spoken the picture of the object should be there in the mind. Sometimes a whole situation may be created. To take the first word *bow*. This might suggest a bow on a child's hair, or shoe-laces tied in a bow, or a cellist or violinist drawing a bow across the strings. Some static picture or situation will develop from the single word into the mind of the speaker, and if vividly imagined will then be transferred in whole or in part to the listener. This is, of course, what happens when matter is read aloud to a listening group, but it can be developed through exercise and brought into control in much the same way as we tackled voice and body. It helps to bring the printed word to life and gives the associated meanings referred to on page 39. If the word so formed in the exercise is an adjective, then the word can be spoken with the appropriate tone colour. If a verb, then the 'action' of the verb can be 'felt' in the voice while the mind imagines the movement, e.g. *slow* or *row*. There may well be more than one meaning attached to the word formed in this way: e.g. if using the vowel *ay*, the word *may* will be made. The word can be spoken as a noun, thinking of the image, and then as a verb on a compound inflection (i.e. the voice moving through a series of notes to suggest uncertainty). This simple exercise should be taken quickly, so that the voice is reacting instinctively and spontaneously to the words presented by the mind. It can be varied enormously by the addition of a final consonant, thus:

Vowel sound *oo*; consonant *m*   Vowel sound *oh*; consonant *t*

boom	*room*		*boat*	*note*
combe	*tomb*		*coat*	*quote*
doom	*womb*		*dote*	*rote*
loom			*goat*	*tote*
			moat	*vote*

I. A. Richards (*op. cit.*) says 'there are no gloomy and no sad vowels or syllables', but an inventive teacher will see great possibilities in this exercise for budding poets in their class. Mere repetition of words ending in *oom* begins to build an atmosphere, and younger children enjoy the use of rhymed words spoken rhythmically. Used as a class exercise it can even form a basis for choral speech or as inarticulate 'sound effects' to support dramatic movement. As there are (omitting *a, e, i, o, u, x*, and *k* – which gives the same sound as *c*) nineteen consonants to be added in various ways to the six long vowel sounds or to the seven short vowel sounds, and, finally, to the diphthongs and triphthongs if necessary, the exercise can be given great variety. However, as with the relaxation and singing exercises, if mental control is the object, then continual repetition is an excellent test of alertness and control. It is relatively easy to be alert with new material. It is much more difficult when the material has become stale: but though stale, therefore a better test. It is, after all, memorised words which are going to be spoken time and time again, and while not sending ourselves mad with too much repetition, we should not give up too easily either. This again is only what scales are to the musician or limbering to the dancer. We need to keep a balance here as in everything else – occasionally some well-worn material, followed by something new, and short daily practice is of far more value than long sessions at erratic intervals.

All the foregoing concerns personal imagery. How much of this do we communicate? Here an interesting class exercise for teachers to develop can be to ask everyone to think up a simple sentence, as short as possible. For example:

'So they killed him.'
'The sheep were in the field.'
'Dawn broke.'

Each speaker will have a full imaginative 'picture' of the background to the sentence, and will imagine this as he speaks the words. The listeners will then be asked to describe what they 'saw' when the words were spoken. To take the first example: 'So they killed him.' What did they see? A firing squad? A crucifixion? A hanging, lynching, drowning? How near are their reactions to the speaker's own imagined scene? The second example might seem more obvious; but how many sheep? Were there trees in the field? Was it the whole field or just one corner of it? Were there any houses in view? What sort of day was it? Finally, 'Dawn broke.' Summer or winter? Was the sky grey or crimson or what? Was there any wind moving the clouds swiftly?

Often a class will be surprised at how much they can transmit in this way, but if the speaker is vividly imagining an experience, a description, or action, the listeners will obtain a very clear and accurate impression if they choose to respond. Obviously this exercise needs concentration and lack of self-consciousness from all involved and honesty from speaker and listener. But it can be a fascinating way of interesting young people or mature students in the power of words to convey thoughts, and can frequently stimulate imaginative thinking. Like all such exercises, it needs presenting with tact and understanding of the basic object, which is still flexibility and control of the mental processes stimulated by language. It should never be overdone, or what we may call 'intrusive imagery' will be the result.

To elaborate on this. In more subtle poetry, the imagery may well be implied and not actual, and for the mind to be conveying pictures indiscriminately could be disastrous. This will happen if the student is overdeveloped imaginatively and possibly underdeveloped intellectually. Speaking poetry he may tend to present a series of isolated and unconnected visual images, which merely confuse the listener. He has probably judged the poem superficially from the words on the page and has failed to see the poet's true purpose. Compare, say, 'The Shell' by James Stephens with C. Day-Lewis's Sonnet No. 1 from 'O Dreams O Destinations'. In the first poem the poet is simply describing what happens when you listen to a sea-shell. He gives the action thus:

> And then I pressed the shell
> Close to my ear
> And listened well. . . .

The speaker will need to have a very vivid picture of the action implied in the words, so that he 'feels' the shell against his ear and 'hears' the sound that it makes. But in the C. Day-Lewis sonnet the poet is comparing two things. He is saying that, as the sound in the sea-shell is to the sea, so infant-time is to the life span which he has to cover.

> For infants, time is like a humming shell
> Heard between sleep and sleep. . . .

It is the whole simile which must be conveyed – not isolated images of shells or of sleep. Another sonnet in this sequence gives a similar example. Sonnet No. 9 starts:

> To travel like a bird, lightly to view
> Deserts where stone gods founder in the sand,
> Oceans embraced in a white sleep with land;
> To escape time, always to start anew. . . .

It is possible to hear students speak this as though the action were happening in actual fact rather than, in this case, the metaphorical comparison of escaping time as a bird escapes from the world into the sky.

Thus we have been working towards mind-dominated relaxation, physical, vocal, and imaginative flexibility and control, with the *emphasis on language as the releasing factor*. The whole body must be employed in the speaking, not just a part. It was Dylan Thomas who suggested that speakers should choose poems which make their toenails twinkle, and this is an excellent image to bear in mind.

Here attention must be drawn to the outstanding results in vocal freedom which can be obtained from wise handling of verbal dynamics, a method created and developed by Jocelyn Bell and Christabel Burniston in their book *Verbal Dynamics*. Handled with care this method has splendid results, and its few dangers are thoroughly examined and dealt with in the book on the subject. Obviously overshading of descriptive words will tend to result in artificiality, and while satiric, narrative, and dramatic poetry can sometimes stand heavier vocal colouring and contrast, lyric poetry requires a delicacy and control which must never be endangered.

To summarise: we work for complete control over our instrument, i.e. mind, body, and voice. We learn to relax in a controlled way in order that nothing shall intrude between us and our subject, and to subdue self to text. The greater the poem the more the speaker must withdraw his own personality. A weaker poem may be given extra weight by a very imaginative speaker who can sometimes supply a quality lacking in the writing. But to speak superb lyric like 'The Salutation' by Thomas Traherne, or any sonnet of Shakespeare, to read Shelley's 'To Night' or Keats's 'Ode to a Nightingale', Matthew Arnold's 'Dover Beach', or Browning's 'Two in the Campagna', or to start to approach the deep insight and mysticism of the poetry of Gerard Manley Hopkins or the Duino Elegies of Rilke or the Four Quartets of T. S. Eliot without immaculate technique, complete concentration, and utter removal of self is to be arrogant indeed. Keats (*The Letters of John Keats*, Ed. Buxton) himself believed that the excellence of an art lay in its intensity. But also that this could not be striven after but must be passively awaited in a state of preparedness. As Keats remarked in a letter:

> Let us not therefore go hurrying here and there impatiently for a knowledge of what is to be aimed at, but let us open our leaves like a flower and be passive and receptive.

Nor in our search must we omit some study of the other arts. As I. A. Richards (*op. cit.*) says:

> Comparison of the arts is, in fact, far the best means by which an understanding of the methods and resources of any one of them can be attained.

Perhaps, too, we may borrow the words of T. S. Eliot in 'East Coker':

> And so each venture
> Is a new beginning, a raid on the inarticulate.

> every attempt
> Is a wholly new start, and a different kind of failure.

We may now consider how best to interest classes and audiences unaccustomed to listening to poetry.

CHAPTER 5

Interpretation I: Poetry of the Present

The Twentieth Century

All waits for the right voices;
Where is the practis'd and perfect organ? where is the developed soul?
For I see every word utter'd thence has deeper, sweeter, new sounds im-
possible on less terms.

(WALT WHITMAN, 'Vocalism'.)

A television programme explored the famous poem 'Tyger, Tyger' by
William Blake, and a child of no more than 8 years spoke the poem with
more understanding of its inner heart and rhythm than could be matched
by the adult actor's voice recorded behind the various pictures offered as
illustration. It was obvious that the child felt the rhythm of the tiger
padding heavy-footed through the jungle, and because she was not
attempting to 'understand' the poem – how could she? – she literally let
the poem speak.

In all the arts we attempt to become as 'little children' and to achieve
thereby the clarity and simplicity which too much knowledge of the
wrong sort will cloud. Therefore the subsequent discussion of specific
poems will be concerned with interpretation rather than with form,
metre, rhythm, etc., since many textbooks already exist which can give all
this information as and when it is required. Knowledge of this sort will
only partially help a speaker to communicate a poem. It will assist his own
understanding of and pleasure from the poem on the page, but just as the
child mentioned above did not need to know that 'tyger' is a trochaic
and not an iambic word, unless a speaker can enter imaginatively into a
poem, such knowledge is of only academic use.

One of the reasons why so few books exist which can help in the speaking of poetry is that it is immensely difficult to convey an abstract quality in the written word. It is so much easier to discuss the literary values of poems or the overall merit of the subject or individual writers than it is to say what we need to do in order to convey these or how we are to go about doing it. When we have heard a poem read well, what remains in our minds? The poem? If the reading was really good we were unaware of the reader. Hence the need for the training already referred to. Why do we not then have only silent reading by individuals in the privacy of their own rooms? Because there are many people who are unable to imagine the sound of words merely by seeing them on the page, and in the last instance it is the sound of poetry which establishes its full sense. Many of these people will never discover poetry unless they hear it first.

So after hearing poetry well read we are left with an experience. It may be pleasant, disturbing, revolting, interesting, or enlightening, or a combination of all these. It may be a descriptive picture which remains in our minds, or a mood, or an idea, or a revelation. It will be concerned with sound, but sound will not be what we remember. If we, as speakers, know what we wish to convey, we are halfway to conveying it. No book of this size can do justice to the immense possibilities in the speaking of poetry and neither space nor copyright will allow inclusion of vast numbers of examples, but the poems to be dealt with in this chapter and some from the following chapter have been recorded. The poems have been grouped round the related themes of births, marriages, deaths, and the Mortal World, and whilst all have been chosen on merit they have also been selected to represent various aspects of interpretation as they affect the speaker. A knowledge of basic prosody has to be assumed and of the rich variety of traditional verse patterns evolved during the last five or six centuries. These are constantly being modified to suit the needs of modern thought and ideas, and there is less concern with established forms in this century than in the past and more experiment with unusual forms and rhythms to suit unusual subject-matter. The essential point for the speaker to remember is that with a good poet the rhythm and form harmonise with the subject-matter. Find the 'heart' of the poem and you will find its 'pulse'. Communicate the poet's intention, once you feel you know what that is, and his means will become your means. Study poetry too much as an abstract 'subject' and you will always be too aware of means as opposed to ends. Learn to see the poem on the page not as a piece of literature only, but as a record of an experience. If we recognise the experience we can then discover what means the poet used to record that experience, and use the same means to communicate this to others.

It seems wise to bring new audiences to poetry through the work of contemporary poets first, since their idiom is familiar and their imagery more immediate. If the present day can be seen to be illuminated by twentieth-century poets in an arresting and stimulating way, there is more likely to be a desire to 'compare and contrast' this with poetry of the past, where the problems will then be found to be the same, though expressed in somewhat differing language.

The first poem to be considered is 'Prayer Before Birth' by Louis MacNeice. This is an incantatory poem spoken by the child in the womb and reminding us of our responsibilities towards the unborn. It also reveals the fact that birth as well as death can be a terrifying thing. The main problem for the speaker is one of overall tone of voice and atmosphere. Obviously any attempt to sound like an unborn child must be doomed to failure, since unborn children do not speak. Should the words therefore be intoned on one flat pitch, as befits a 'Prayer'? This can have the effect of riveting attention on manner rather than on matter and seems to work against the very considerable strength and force of the chosen words. Therefore it seems necessary to allow these words to dominate and to concentrate on removal of personality altogether so that the delivery has the impersonality of a non-person, which in fact is what it is. So the removal of self here is not to assume the persona of the poet, but to allow his language to work unadorned and unhampered, a very good first example of 'letting the poem speak'.

But 'letting the poem speak' does not mean doing no preparation at all and merely voicing the poem and leaving the listeners to make what they can of it. It means considering very deeply before the speaking begins the full range, scope, and variety of horrors, fears, and joys which are going to be experienced by this as yet unborn member of the human race. The fears and fancies build up to a climax at the words

> Let not the man who is beast or who thinks he is God
> Come near me;

The extremes of height and depth. The rest is really almost a running-down of impetus with the appeal not to be 'dissipated', not to be 'dragooned into a lethal automaton'; not to be 'blown about like thistledown', etc. But despair is there behind the words. There is little feeling that the prayer will be answered. Instead there is almost resignation that it will not. So the final lines,

> Let them not make me a stone and let them not spill me.
> Otherwise kill me

cannot justifiably be made too dramatic but rather a flat acceptance of what must be. Yet the poem is obviously dramatic and it is written in the first person, so the speaker must experience the horrors behind the reading or the poem becomes just a catalogue of possible disasters, somewhat contrived and unconvincing. It has been spoken, chanted, intoned, and recorded in many different ways, and its great merit is that it transcends its own period and becomes more and more meaningful as time goes on, rather as Huxley's 'Brave New World' or Orwell's '1984'.

It is written out on the page in a very interesting shape, and will therefore serve to introduce a point of essential technique which applies to all speaking.

Every line of spoken poetry requires an end-of-line pause to preserve the SHAPE of the poem as it appears on the page, but if the sense runs on – enjambment – then the end-of-line pause is not required and it is then replaced by a suspensory pause, the voice being suspended through holding the final consonant or vowel fractionally longer than is absolutely necessary. For example:

> 'I am not yet born: O hear me.
> Let not the bloodsucking bat or the rat or the stoat or the club-footed ghoul
>   come near me.

This has the effect of throwing attention on to the words which follow, since pause is always a means of emphasis. Thus the 'club-footed ghoul' stands out very slightly from the general list of undesirable creatures since there must be a slight pause after it; also to preserve rhythm, the phrase 'come near me' balancing the words 'O hear me' in the previous line. (This is an example of a caesura or sense-pause which helps convey meaning and divides phrases where there is no punctuation.) Similarly, in stanza 3 of the same poem we have

> I am not yet born; provide me
> with water to dandle me, grass to grow for me, trees to talk
> to me, sky to sing to me, birds and a white light
> in the back of my mind to guide me.

(The white light could have been in the sky, but the pause establishes that it is to be in the mind as a guide.) These final words all carry a suspensory pause – suspend the *ee* of 'me', the *awk* of 'talk', the final *t* of 'light' for just a fraction of a second longer than is absolutely necessary in order to preserve the poem's shape and give slight added significance to the words which follow. This also adds strength and variety to the overall reading and obeys the poet's purpose since he would not have written his poem in that particular shape had he not required emphasis at those points. The classic example of this occurs in T. S. Eliot's 'Journey of the Magi' when he gives immense strength to an instruction thus:

> But set down
> *This* set down
> *This*.

Spoken without the suspensory pause the poem would only say 'But set down this set down this'.

A poet's punctuation is always important; and perhaps the most difficult mark of all for the speaker to deal with is the comma. This should occasion a slight pause but no dropping of the voice since the sense has not ended. If the voice drops at a comma, at a semi-colon, at a colon, and finally at a full stop, the reading has continual dying falls which can be both monotonous and melancholy. 'Prayer Before Birth' needs a sense of mounting tension and climax if it is to hold the interest of the listener since it is composed of lists of possible situations, e.g. stanza 5:

> old men lecture me, bureaucrats hector me, mountains
> frown at me, lovers laugh at me, the white
> waves call me to folly and the desert calls
> me to doom and the beggar refuses
> my gift and my children curse me.

If the commas are used as just a slight suspension the tension mounts, and so does the pace as the commas give way and only the line ends are left with their suspensory pauses. The tiny sense pauses at the word 'and' will in each case enable breath to be taken in through the mouth. The mouth opens to say 'and', and breath is thus replenished. This so-called 'snatched breath' is essential when speaking at speed, and gathering up pace is very necessary here since it is building to the climax mentioned earlier which occurs in the next stanza.

In this way and through the symbols on the page the poet imposes his will on the reader, who must then fit himself to the poem, not the poem to himself. Unfortunately it is still possible to find actors, both amateur and professional, who think nothing of repunctuating a poem to suit their own needs, often ignoring line-ends altogether and endeavouring to make the work sound as much like prose as possible, feeling perhaps that this is more 'natural'.

In general terms, therefore, the voice pauses only at a comma, falls slightly at a semi-colon, somewhat more at a colon, and finally descends fully at a full stop. Even full stops should have a variety of notes to which the voice can descend depending on the finality of the matter, and this does begin to reveal the necessity for full vocal control.

To show the importance of noting a poet's punctuation, here is a poem in which the sense is entirely altered by the varied use of comma, semi-colon, colon, and full stop.

At the World's End

by JOHN SMITH

At the world's end nothing,
  Not a sound, not a sigh;
The vivid landscape
  That painted the eye
    Gone into space,
    Not a scratch, not a trace;
At the world's end, nothing.

At the world's end, nothing?
  Then why, love, why
Such tears, such lamenting?
  What use is the cry
    Of the heart? It will seem
    But a fitful dream
At the world's end: nothing.

At the world's end, nothing
  My dear, my dear,
Will redeem that loss
  As our love here:
    That alone will not be
    Like you, like me,
At the world's end, nothing.

The first stanza states that at the end of the world there will be nothing. The second stanza then says why should lovers dread the end of the world since all life will seem then like a dream? The third stanza says that love in this world will make up for the fact that there is nothing to go on to in the next. All this is achieved in the most economical way by the use of punctuation to alter subtly the recurring line 'At the world's end nothing', since in each stanza the inflection of the voice must change as required by the placing of either comma, question mark, colon, or full stop, and by the use of enjambment in stanza 3. The run-on lines necessitate use of a suspensory pause to keep the poem's shape and to give emphasis to the rhymed words which occur in a regular rhyme scheme of ABCBDDA.

In any speaking a pause is always necessary at the end of a stanza, since this again fulfils the poet's intention. Had he not wanted a break he would not have divided his poem into stanzas. Frequently these denote a change or development of mood or idea, and the audience needs time to take in what has already gone and prepare for that which is to come. It is noticeable that a quicker reading is possible if the listeners are following a text, since their eyes are assisting their ears, and this factor should be taken into consideration when preparing the work.* Without a text the matter will be taken in by the ear only, and this matter needs time to 'digest' before more matter is offered for consumption. An accustomed or quick audience needs less time obviously than an unaccustomed or slow audience, and the speaker will adjust according to the response which he feels is being manifest (see Chapter 3). On the other hand, a too slow reading can stretch the matter beyond its own rhythmic structure, and this will lessen the poem's impact.

A third poem will show this: 'Morning Song' by Sylvia Plath. This is a simple poem about the actual birth of a child. But within the prosaic language there lies the whole wonder and amazement of having created another human being. You make love and incidentally you make another person. 'Love set you going like a fat gold watch'.

What a perfect and unusual simile. From then on all the imagery is concerned with the immenseness of the world and the marvellous process of birth compared with the smallness of those who become involved. The baby is likened to a 'new statue in a drafty museum' – the mother to no more than 'the cloud that distils a mirror to reflect its own slow / Effacement at the wind's hand.' Those involved 'stand round blankly as walls'. The baby's open mouth is described as 'clean as a cat's' – this simile involving the whole of the natural world of feeding mammals. There is undoubtedly a sense of wonder behind all the words, yet the surface of the

---

* This is particularly true in broadcasting where the producer needs to listen to rehearsal without a text himself in order to adjust the timing of his readers to the needs of their audience – essential in unpublished work. In recordings which are going to be played many times, a delivery fully up to time is desirable or the work loses the spontaneity of natural speech and can sound over-explained. These differences are fractional but essential.

poem is pervaded by humour and naturalness which must dominate the delivery. The reading needs the flow and fluency of natural discourse with the sense of wonder behind the words. If this inner heart is concentrated upon during the speaking, there will be less reverence to actual words and more to emotional experience. 'Morning Song' could be spoken with hushed, awed reverence, but this would work against the texture of the words and would lose the essential atmosphere of the poem, which is of deep feelings hidden behind commonplace actions and an almost flippant verbal expression. Conversely a flat prosaic reading only would not do, since if there were no indication of deeper feelings, the listener might well wonder why the poet bothered to write the poem at all. So while the 'essence' of the poem is that of wonder, the expression of that wonder is almost 'matter-of-fact'.

This underlines the need to memorise a poem at some stage. Words which are spoken 'by heart' (not such a misnomer really) frequently reveal the 'heart' of the matter in a way never quite matched by a reading, because the printed symbols are bound to intrude, even if only slightly. Of course, the more technically able the speaker the more he can afford to concentrate on the poem's essence. If any part of his mind is having to think of the breath or emphasis, rhythm or relaxation, or even the words, these extraneous thoughts must weaken his communication.

So the overall atmosphere of any poem is immensely important. It is necessary to think of this before beginning to read. To pause momentarily to consider the mood, situation, emotion, or period of both poem and poet. Sometimes the title can help to establish the poem, and the speaking of this will prepare both audience and speaker for the poem which is to follow – 'Prayer Before Birth' and 'Morning Song' can certainly help in this way. Certainly to start with a wrong or uncertain atmosphere is very unnerving and difficult to correct, since concentration is already disturbed. So a pause before and after the title will set the mood, and this is as necessary in a light and cheerful poem as it is in a more sombre or serious one.

It cannot be too often emphasised that if the thought is right the rhythm of speech and the tone will be right. 'Take care of the thought and

the words will take care of themselves' might be an adapted maxim for all
verse speakers. The already-mentioned 'poetry voice' was often caused by
over-reverence for the material. Many speakers feel such a tremendous
respect for the poem they are about to speak that they become tentative,
feeling that they cannot possibly do justice to the poet's words. This gives
the breathy hushed tone which is so artificial and embarrassing to the
listener. The speaker can appear to be 'two feet off the ground' and to
assume an ecstatic facial expression which is frequently at a complete
variance with the poem being read. As an anonymous writer once
remarked: poetry should be read:

> Not in the dull sepulchral tones
> The well trained elocutionist owns,
> But as a poem should be read
> To the living – not the dead!

The heart of a poem can be precisely the same whether expressed in
eighteenth- or twentieth-century language. Consider, for instance, 'Infant
Joy' by William Blake and 'Born Yesterday' by Phillip Larkin. Both are
wishing happiness to a newly born child. But how different is their mode
of expression. The Blake poem has the newly born child speaking:

> 'I have no name.
> I am but two days old.'
> 'What shall I call thee?'
> 'I happy am,
> Joy is my name.'
> 'Sweet joy befall thee.'

In the Larkin poem the poet speaks to the 'tightly folded bud' and in plain
language he says the same thing. The only time the language becomes at
all highly charged is in the last four lines:

> In fact, may you be dull –
> If that is what a skilled,
> Vigilant, flexible,
> Unemphasised, enthralled –
> Catching of happiness is called.

A student could speak the Phillip Larkin poem with little difficulty and no embarrassment but might feel wary of the Blake. Yet wishing happiness to a child is a most natural and simple thing, and speaking the two poems one after the other and concentrating on their 'message' rather than on their language brings home the point that language and intention are one and the same thing. It is therefore as 'natural' to say 'I happy am, / Joy is my name', if you are thinking right, as it is to say 'In fact, may you be dull', etc. In the Blake poem there has to be a slight contrast in the 'voices' of the adult and the child, but this is merely achieved through thinking and not through any conscious attempt to 'characterise'. The younger voice will automatically take a slightly higher pitch, but again any attempt to sound like a 2-day-old child would obviously be ridiculous since 2-day-old children do not articulate. Modern listeners will 'suspend their disbelief' if the thinking is right, and will accept the eighteenth-century poem as readily as the modern one.*

This kind of comparison can be useful in introducing students to poetry of the past, and to traditional forms, e.g. the Sonnet.† Examination of the form here is not concerned with its literary value, but its difficulties for the speaker, difficulties occasioned by its compactness and its fourteen-line brevity.

A sonnet is the ultimate in distilled thought, the final summary of intense speculation and meditation, and therefore the speaker has to do a great deal of mental work to discover just how this final distillation was arrived at. Then he, too, must condense his thinking to exactly match his speaking – a difficult task since the thinking also has to be matched to the deca-syllabic lines and to the rhyme scheme. Mention has already been made of the superb recordings of Shakespeare's sonnets by Sir John Gielgud, but no amount of listening to Sir John will alter the fact that every student must do his own thinking as he will have to do his own speaking.

Petrachan and Shakespearean sonnets will be discussed further in the following chapter, but students may well find it easier to speak these if there has been some earlier experience of modern sonnets, particularly if

---

* This point is developed in the following chapter.
† For information of the origin and development the reader is directed to *The English Sonnet* by B. Crutwell (Longmans).

they are part of a sonnet sequence. One such is C. Day-Lewis's sequence of nine titled 'O Dreams O Destinations', in which he compares the promise of infancy and youth to the realisation of adulthood. (Other examples are W. H. Auden's 'Journey to a War', or George Meredith's 'Modern Love' – though the latter has a sixteen-line instead of a fourteen-line form).

In 'O Dreams O Destinations' there are nine sonnets, and it is helpful to speak these in order as though each one were a complete stanza of a long poem. This encourages the feeling of one idea in each fourteen lines and prevents the individual sonnets from sounding like well-reasoned debating points. It forces more compact thought and disciplines the delivery into the required shape. In other forms of verse speaking care has to be taken not to anticipate the end of the poem at the beginning, since most poems reflect some variety of mood, however subtle. In a sonnet, however, it is necessary to have gathered up the whole poem before the speaking begins in order to convey its intensity.

In its original form devised by the Italian Petrach, it divided into octave (first eight lines) and sestet (last six); statement and development, and its rhyme scheme was ABBA, ABBA, EFG EFG (or EFE, FEF, or EF EF EF), but because of the difficulty of rhyming in the English language, it was adapted into ABAB, CDCD, EFEF, GG, and here the couplet at the end is the climax and ultimate conclusion of the thought. Therefore according to the form the sonnet will be spoken either with a slight pause at the end of the eighth line to mark the climax, or with a slight pause before the final couplet. This essential structure must be incorporated into the thinking. Thus in the first of the Day-Lewis sequence the sonnet builds up to the final couplet, which says of infants:

> They are the lisping rushes in a stream –
> Grace notes of a profound, legato dream.

If spoken after a slight pause, the couplet will retain spontaneity – as though it had just that moment been created in the mind – and will round off the matter.

In the deepest emotions there is the least action, e.g. joy, grief, terror.

Similarly in the sonnet there is intensity of thought and correspondingly small vocal movement. This is not to suggest that all sonnets are of equal profundity of subject-matter – the one quoted is a simple simile as described in Chapter 4, yet the speaking of such sonnets will prepare for the more complex and therefore more rewarding ones to come.

Mention of poetic form and intensity can occasion some discussion of a little-used form selected by Dylan Thomas to express his feelings on the impending death of his father. The poem 'Do Not Go Gentle into that Good Night' – the form, the Villanelle. The definition of this form is as follows. It has five stanzas, each of three lines, followed by one stanza of four lines. It has a refrain which consists of the first and third lines of the first stanza. These lines alternately form the last lines of the four middle stanzas, and reappear as a concluding couplet to the poem. Only two rhymes are employed throughout. Stanzas one to five rhyme ABA and stanza six ABAA, by which it will be seen to be a highly disciplined and difficult form in which to fit a deeply felt emotion. Yet it is surely for this reason that Dylan Thomas chose it for one of his strongest and most powerful poems. As with a sonnet, it is impossible to be superficial when reading this poem. It forces one to weigh and consider every single word, and, as with all refrains, the constant repetition builds up an almost un-bearable tension and poignancy of emotion. It must go at speed or the force of repetition is slackened and loses its effect, and it must be spoken with complete conviction.

Some people find difficulty here since they will argue that it is absurd to rail against the inevitability of death. But speaking the poem reveals the absolute integrity of the poet, who is offering himself as a bulwark against the distress of the dying father. How many of us confronted with a dying man wish the death to be swift and painless for our own sakes. How many of us can face up to the fact that many people do not want to die, do not 'go gentle into that good night'. It seems obvious that Dylan Thomas is not saying fight against dying at all costs, but saying if you want to make a fuss, then make it to me and I will understand and help you to bear the pain. He makes the point that no one, however wise or informed, can say for certain how he will behave when death advances. Neither 'wise men' nor 'good men' nor 'wild men' nor 'grave men', so his own father can be said to be in good company and should feel no shame at his 'fierce tears'. It is a profoundly moving poem and its form is perfectly matched to its intense feeling.

When speaking it the repetition feels akin to the inability of human beings to communicate in moments of great stress other than by constantly saying the same thing over and over again, the brain presumably being somewhat numbed by the shock of the emotion. Very different from certain purple passages of grand rhetoric in verse plays, when intellect murmurs that such verbal fluency would be unlikely in such circumstances. An equivalent difficulty is experienced by those encountering operatic arias for the first time. There has to be acceptance of the limitations or releases of the medium in all instances, and though the poem may seem nearer to reality by virtue of its brevity, it is of course equally unlikely that one would speak such a highly disciplined form at such a moment. But 'art is art because it is not life'. It 'holds up a mirror to nature', and certainly this poem extends the speaker spiritually as well as vocally.

This form, together with the triolet, rondeau, ballade, and sestina, were originally of French origin, and as with the sonnet, the difficulty of rhyming in the English language has led to many variations being presented. For the speaker the poet's reason for choice of form is most important, as is appreciation of the devices he uses within the chosen form, and the speaker will explore all these in his preparation of the poem. But once the speaking starts the 'means' should be completely subservient to the 'ends'. Wherever a refrain occurs, as it does with all the above except the sestina, it should be allowed to do its work of emphasis. It does not require, as many speakers seem to think, constant variety. Its sameness is its strength. To take another example on the subject of death, 'The Gallows' by Edward Thomas. This is an adapted form of ballad. It has four stanzas of eight lines, all concluding with the line – 'On the dead oak tree bough'.

The preceding lines are varied on the theme 'without pleasure, without pain', in the first and third stanza, changing to 'There are no more sins to be sinned' in the second stanza, and reversing to 'Without pain, without pleasure' in the final stanza. Each stanza is rhymed to ABABCDCD and the poem gathers momentum by its repeated rhythmical refrain and the similarity of its fourth lines:

Where he swings in the wind and rain (Verse 1).
To hang and flap in rain and wind (Verse 2).
He, too, flaps in the wind and rain (Verse 3).
To swing and have endless leisure (Verse 4).

The poet therefore achieves the feeling of the universality of death which must come to all creatures, and gives a descriptive picture of the slow swinging on the 'dead oak tree bough' through the rhythmic pattern of 'to and fro' which is consistent throughout.

Another form of repetition popular in the 'House-that-Jack-built' type of nursery rhyme is the building up of lines to the climax line which is repeated every time. Robert Graves adapted this in his 'Warning to Children' with its immensely suggestive 'poem within a poem' type of approach. The 'refrain' the first time is in the present tense:

Blocks of slate enclosing dappled
Red and green, enclosing tawny
Yellow nets, enclosing white
And black acres of dominoes.

This then goes into the past tense on its second appearance:

Blocks of slate enclosed by dappled
Red and green, enclosed by tawny
Yellow nets, enclosed by white
And black acres of dominoes.

On its third appearance it then reverses to:

Blocks of slate about his head
Find himself enclosed by dappled
Green and *red*, enclosed by *yellow*
Tawny nets, enclosed by *black*
And *white* acres of dominoes.

The poem begins and ends with the reversed phrases of 'greatness, rareness, muchness, fewness', 'fewness, muchness, rareness, greatness', which gives a very satisfying 'order out of chaos' feeling to the listener – a point mentioned in Chapter 1. Again the speaker is aware of these devices but will not force or over-emphasise them in the speaking, since they do their own work of emphasis without added vocal assistance.

Where there does need to be some vocal assistance is in the speaking of humorous, satiric, dramatic, and narrative verse, and the big question always is, How much assistance is really helpful? How dramatic should a dramatic poem be? How much 'pointing' should a humorous or satiric poem need? Once again it must be a matter of intention – the poet's intention.

It is always awkward to endeavour to divide poetry into unnatural headings of lyric/narrative, lyric/dramatic, dramatic/narrative, etc., since much lyric poetry can have a narrative or even a dramatic streak, and much narrative is lyric in tone and so on.* The dictionary meaning of 'dramatic' gives 'fit for theatrical representation; sudden, striking, impressive (of utterances, etc.); not to be taken as one's own, representing another person's thoughts' – the latter in this context is interesting. If the poet actually speaks with another person's voice in his poem, then there must be some characterisation or the speaking will lack contrast and the character will lack life. For example, John Betjeman's atmospheric little poem 'Death in Leamington'. Here the poet describes with all his usual brilliant economy the pathetic death of an old lady in an upstairs bedroom in Leamington Spa. The room with its air of decaying gentility, its very smell of age, is perfectly created in the first two four-line stanzas. Then the poet introduces a second character, the trained nurse, and she speaks to the old lady who is already dead.

> 'AND Tea!' she said in a tiny voice
> 'Wake up! It's nearly five.'

There is a precise instruction in the 'tiny voice', and the following lines continue the instruction with:

> Oh! chintzy, chintzy cheeriness,
> Half dead and half alive.

---

* See *The Speaking of Poetry* by Geoffrey Crump, Dobson Books, where this point is developed.

So we are left in no doubt as to the kind of person she is, and as we 'see' her so we must 'hear' her, and her voice must be 'tiny' and desperately 'cheery' in our reading of the poem. But this characterisation must be gently done or it will overweigh the poem and make nurse the central character, since the emphasis will be thrown on the change of voice, whereas, of course, the old lady in the bed is what must remain in the listener's mind.

In a poem of this nature we are working on a small canvas and need the delicacy of water-colourists rather than the bold sweep of an oil-painter, remembering always that the poet is a master in the choice of words and any heavy-handedness of delivery will detract by overweighting. Sometimes the 'characters' take over the whole poem and the effect then is of a dramatic monologue rather than a poem. But as Kenneth Tynan points out in *Curtains*, 'A playwright is a man who can forget himself long enough to be other people, and a poet is a man who can forget other people long enough to be himself.'

Therefore a poem like Paul Roche's 'Metathalamium', while it must bring to life the whole sad scene of the incompatible couple after twelve years of marriage, is still nevertheless a poem and does not need 'acting up' to make its points. All its images, for example, are so perfectly chosen to complement the moods they illustrate. The wife is 'filing her fingertips' and 'picks up her knitting' – the sharp venom of her frustrated sexual passions is literally 'pointed' by these two actions. The husband kicks her shoes, drags at the bedclothes, punches her pillow, but cannot bring himself to hit out at her, which is what she needs. The poem grips the imagination and we feel the pain of both wife and husband in equal measure. In equal measure? This must be qualified. The poem is written by a man and the husband would seem to have the poet's sympathy, but no woman reading it could fail to have sympathy also for the wife, and this would seem to be the poet's intention: to hold the balance and not to sit in judgement.

But it does bring up the interesting comparisons between men and women reading the same poem. However much the personality of the speaker is withdrawn, it is still through one's own intellectual mechanism

that the poet and his poem are seen. Therefore there cannot really fail to
be some slight shift of emphasis, and this makes masculine and feminine
interpretations of the same poem so interesting. An example of this
occurs in Sir Philip Sidney's sonnet 'Loving in Truth'. In the last lines
he says:

> Thus great with child to speak and helpless in my throes,
> Biting my truant pen, beating myself for spite.
> 'Fool,' said my Muse to me, 'look in thy heart and write.'

'Great with child' spoken by a man is a mere metaphor; spoken by a
woman it can become a physical fact. But one of the most remarkable
things about poets is their ability to transcend mere sex, and though slight
shifts of emphasis there may well be, the poem's 'essence'* will still be the
factor to be communicated.†

Finally to humorous or satiric verse. There is sometimes scepticism
among non-performers that comedy is really more difficult than tragedy,
yet the fact remains that this is true. That an amateur company of actors
are more likely to give entertainment to their audience with a comedy than
with a tragedy does not alter the case. Tragedy can be communicated by
sincerity. Comedy needs technique. Similarly with verse. It also needs a
sense of humour, though satire particularly may be deeply serious. Any
attempt to be 'funny' in humorous verse must fail because once again
manner is dominating matter. It is in the subtle 'pointing' of words,
phrases or whole lines, and in the timing, that humour will be communicated, and in the use of the 'throw away'.

'Pointing' is achieved by a tiny pause before and sometimes also after
the word, phrase, or line requiring to be pointed. The length of pause
depends on the degree of pointing required, and within the framework of
a humorous poem there needs to be infinite variety of pointing, or this in
itself becomes monotonous. Hence the need for 'throw away'. If attention
has been drawn to humorous ideas through pointing, and then suddenly
one equally amusing image is allowed to be glossed over, this again is a
means of emphasis and will cause laughter by its underplaying. Not that

---

* See Chapter 2.

† Narrative poetry will be dealt with more fully in the following chapter.

poetry is ever really a comic art. There are very few poems which cause bursts of laughter. Mostly they produce a wry smile or a chuckle, the humour being subtle rather than broad. Of course, their position in a programme can occasion 'relief' laughter, sometimes out of all proportion to the worth of the humour. But this is a reaction against intense concentration (see Chapter 8). To take two poems by Vernon Scannell as illustration; the first is given here in full with the poet's permission, since its source may be difficult to trace (*Poetry Review*, Summer 1965).

The Lady and the Gipsy

I handed her my silver
And gullibility,
And tremulously asked her
Who would marry me,
For I was getting older,
Approaching twenty-three—
At least that's what I told her:
All girls, I'm sure, agree
It's sometimes right to suffer
Lapse of memory.

She told me to be patient,
But not for very long,
For down the summer pavement
As lilting as a song
Mr. Right would wander,
Eager, gallant, strong;
And sure enough last summer
My man did come along:
If he is Mr. Right, then
Give me Mr. Wrong.

To analyse any poem of this nature must seem heavy-handed indeed, but it does need some pointing. The end-of-line pauses and the pause between stanzas will allow all the irony in the first stanza to sink in. Now the pace must gather up with growing excitement right down to 'My man did come along'. Short pause and complete change of tone from lyrical expectation to disgruntled disappointment. Any anticipation of the end will ruin the effect, as will any suggestion in the tone that 'here is a funny poem', or any knowing look on the face. A serious engagement in the situation is essential or the denouement will fall flat.

A second poem, 'Six Year Darling', has a debunking flavour and is written in blank verse, no doubt as an ironic comment on the poets of the past, and this gives the poem a satisfying formality suitable to its subject. It starts rather wryly and sardonically but finishes with a serious comment on childhood, i.e. that perhaps its worst feature is boredom. This could make an interesting talking point, since boredom in childhood is presumably dependent on home and school influence and on the child himself. Any artist will tend to express himself subjectively, and it may be that Wordsworth, Vaughan, Millais, and Milne, who are mentioned in the poem, all had ideal childhoods, and while the main point of the poem is that youth is not of itself ideal, we may feel that it is sad to think of boredom being the dominating memory of childhood. This poem, therefore, serves to illustrate two earlier points. It tells us something about the poet which may well illuminate our further reading of his work. Secondly, the poem reveals how necessary it is to read poet and poem, since many of us cannot remember boredom in childhood, and if we read the poem 'as ourselves' we shall not be 'speaking true', we shall be speaking false and limiting ourselves to the relatively few poems which come within our actual experience. The poetry of Vernon Scannell makes an immediate appeal to audiences of all ages, since it contains understanding of and compassion for human frailties, is frequently spiced with wit – he has a particular talent for excellent and telling final lines – and he deals with contemporary subjects without being too tied to one generation. He acknowledges a great debt to W. H. Auden and possesses much of his neatness of form, and his war poetry has been ranked with that of Wilfred Owen.

The last poem to be discussed reveals the zaniness of Stevie Smith in 'My Hat'. This really gathers up all the points of narrative, dramatic, and humorous verse. The poem is a narrative, i.e. it tells a story; it is dramatic and written in the first person; and it is humorous in its language and in its final line. It is, of course, adult sophisticated humour. Children tend to

take it quite seriously, as they do the poetry of Hilaire Belloc. After all, to
be carried away by a hat is a serious situation, as is 'Matilda's' in being
burned to death. Adults laugh at the contrast between fact and fantasy, at
the underlying Freudian significance of wanting to be rid of 'Father,
Mother, and the Young Man', and at the rhyming. Again this poem needs
speaking with utter seriousness but with some feeling for the oddness of
the character, a somewhat strange creature to whom such an adventure
could happen. Then, as in the Vernon Scannell poem, a change of tone in
the final line and a careful marking of the precise punctuation all through
will add to the 'oddness'. As listeners we must become involved with that
girl, we must 'see' the hat, and sense the 'lifting up' when it happens,
together with the quite lyrical description of the flight and the mysterious-
ness of the island.

Finally, a brief word on imagery. Modern imagery can seem banal when
it is really accurate, factual and topical. For example: Sylvia Plath's 'Love
set you going like a fat gold watch'; Vernon Scannell's '. . . all the illu-
strations are as false / As muscle builders' ads'. These similes immediately
conjure up the required picture in the mind. Yet it is surprising how many
readers and teachers are still rooted in a more traditional imagery which
can blind them to the vividness of such lines from 'Timothy Winters' by
Charles Causley:

> Timothy Winters comes to school
> With eyes as wide as a football pool.

The football is round, the pool is shining, and so are Timothy Winter's
eyes, while the football pool coupon, with its unknown promise, its O's
and X's, is something known to most schoolboys. Brian Patten's

> John sits and he quietly cries
> Tears as big as a choir boy's eyes

from 'Delicate John' has something of the same quality, and in the poem
called 'Seascape' he says:

> you answer with silence
> as tears drip from
> the roof of your womb.

This has been criticised as being very inaccurate, and yet moisture secreted can be likened to tears, so why should not the womb be said to drip tears as naturally as the eyes? It is original and arresting, and if a trifle too arresting for the poem which contains it, at least it has the great merit of originality and jolts the mind into thinking along new lines.

In *The Estate of Poetry* Edwin Muir deplored what he felt to be the lack of balance in modern times between poetic imagination and scientific development and intellect, pointing out that the real strain of modern life is not so much a sense of too much happening too quickly, but of something lacking. Poetry still supplies something of this lack, and constantly uses language in an original and arresting way to keep pace with scientific development.

Can man survive modern scientific horrors, and are these horrors any more horrific than, say, Shakespeare's

> Fear no more the lightning flash
> Nor the all-dread thunder-stone.

His prayer is:

> No exorciser harm thee
> Nor no witchcraft charm thee
> Ghost unlaid forbear thee
> Nothing ill come near thee,

which reminds again of Louis MacNeice's 'Let not the bloodsucking bat or the rat or the stoat or the club-footed ghoul come near me.'

Horrors there are in any age and modern poetry reflects this fact as it reflects also the joys. Perhaps we can now consider some of the poetry of the past, and the difficulties and rewards there for the speaker.

CHAPTER 6

Interpretation II: Poetry of the Past

Pre-twentieth Century

Armies, ships, antiquities, libraries, paintings, machines, cities, hate, despair,
amity, pain, theft, murder, aspirations form in close ranks.
They debouch as they are wanted to march obediently through the mouth
of that man or that woman.

(WALT WHITMAN, 'Vocalism'.)

Now that so many poets are reading their own work so splendidly, both live and on recordings, there is a vital need for teachers and readers to balance the modern viewpoint with poetry of the past. It has been said that imagination is always conservative and this may mean that we all have a unity in imagination which enables writers to write in an endless repetition of a single pattern. As Edwin Muir says in his book *The Estate of Poetry,*

> Poetry will not truly be contemporary or truly poetry, if it deals merely with the immediately perceived contemporary world as if that existed by itself, and were isolated from all that preceded it. It is in the timeless world of the imagination that all generations can meet.

How then do we approach the poetry of the past? Before speaking it do we attempt to imagine ourselves back in time by steeping our consciousness in data appertaining to that period? However well informed we thus become, can we ever seriously believe in what we are attempting? Are we not bound to be regarding the past through the eyes of the present?

An actor playing in a period other than his own must identify himself with the people of that time since he will be wearing their clothes, adopting their manners, stance, customs, and courtesies, and playing against a simulation of their furniture and décor. He will also be speaking in their idiom. Where there has been insufficient research and/or imaginative involvement on the part of director and players, the actors can appear to be wearing fancy dress and reciting language which seems far removed from their actual being. 'No sense of period', say the critics. Yet no one really knows how people from another period actually looked and behaved. What the critics really mean is that there is no synchronisation of thought to speech or to movement, and therefore the piece lacks 'truth' – it is not quite believable.

The speaker of poetry from the past is using an outdated idiom, and to be believable he must also achieve a synchronisation between thought and language. It is an immense help to have studied period movement, and here again the actor speaking verse has an advantage since training in this subject forms part of the curriculum of most academies. There is no doubt that to put on, say, a Victorian crinoline, bonnet, and ringlets is more likely to induce the sort of atmosphere required to speak Elizabeth Barrett Browning than slacks and a sweater, and certainly the speaking of Byron seems to call for the velvet suit and frilly shirt now coming back into fashion. No amount of 'dressing up' will obviate the need for imaginative thinking, and if there is truly imaginative thinking, then the dressing up is unnecessary. But with the best will in the world even imagination needs something to feed on from time to time. We cannot just 'imagine' what the Victorians wore. We need to see pictures, feel materials, and suffer the constriction of corset and crinoline before we can then imagine ourselves to be wearing them.

Similarly we cannot just imagine the political, social, and personal background of a poem. We need some knowledge of these to modify our modern thinking so that we can appreciate some of the strains and tensions, difficulties and joys from which that poem sprang. Basic emotions are common to all men in all ages, e.g. love, fear, hate, happiness, joy, nostalgia, loneliness, grief, etc., but the expression of these varies with each generation. Some people will argue that the poem says all and that there is therefore no need of any background knowledge of either poet or period before the speaking of the poem can be attempted. This can be true of some poetry. Perhaps a perfect lyric does not require any further knowledge. In the case of anonymous writers it has to be true, though the century from which they came is usually known. But many poems, not necessarily so perfect or complete, urge the reader to inquire further into the nature of the writers, as Chapter 2 attempted to show, and do thereby deepen appreciation of what has been attempted, however imperfectly (see Chapter 8). The causes of the attempt may in themselves reveal subtleties otherwise hidden. Just as in the poem by Sylvia Plath there had to be examination of the wonder and awe of which the words were the end product, so in the speaking of a poem from another period the mind will attempt to absorb something of the flavour of that period before the words are spoken. It is a question of imaginative re-creation.

We all feel joy, for example, however briefly, but not all of us remember to store up the memory in our minds and literally practise re-creating the precise physical sensation of that emotional state. Actors are trained to do this, and to realise that everything they do even during a commonplace day can be harnessed to the service of some future imaginative need. Verse speakers need to do this too, and to add to the basic human emotion they are attempting to communicate something of the modifying effect of their knowledge of the period from which it sprang. Then, as Ben Jonson says in 'The Triumph' [recorded], it is possible to say with true delight:

> Have you seen but a bright lily grow
> Before rude hands have touch'd it?
> Have you mark'd but the fall of the snow
> Before the soil hath smutch'd it?
>
> Have you felt the wool of beaver,
> Or swan's down ever?
> Or have smelt of the bud of the brier,
> Or the nard in the fire?
> Or have tasted the bag of the bee?
> Oh so white, O so soft, O so sweet is she,

and to feel that this is a perfectly natural comparison with the beloved.

Thus we, as speakers, exercising our own imaginative powers triggered off by the poet's words, are enriching our own lives beyond measure and attempting to communicate some of this richness to others.

The first difficulty, then, is the actual language. To some students even to have to say 'How do I love *thee*', rather than 'How do I love *you*' is immediately awkward and unnatural. We do not use 'thee' in modern communication – we use 'you'. (The line comes, of course, from Elizabeth Barrett Browning's Sonnet No. 43 – 'Sonnets from the Portuguese'.) If this sonnet is given a completely modern reading there will instantly be a dichotomy between style and language, no synchronisation, and therefore only partial belief. If the reading is to be recorded or broadcast and the speaker has full imaginative involvement with the period, then the listeners will create for themselves the appearance of Victoriana. In a reading composed of many periods it is obviously not either possible or desirable to 'dress the part' in actual fact, but there can be some imaginative readjustment in the mind of the reader from period and period, and dress forms a part of this readjustment. Then, depending on the nature of the poem, other background knowledge can be filled in.

In discussing specific examples of poetry of the past, we may well begin with the sonnet, working backwards, so to speak, from the modern versions touched on in the previous chapter.

The most perfect versions of what came to be known as the Shakespearean form are to be found, somewhat naturally, in the 154 written by Shakespeare himself. Once again more books have been written about these than one could enumerate, so from the speaker's point of view just one will be taken as an example. As already mentioned, the original Italian form as used by Petrach and called by his name Petrachan, was adapted from octave and sestet to be twelve decasyllabic lines plus a final couplet, rhymed ABABCDCDEFEF GG. If we take the well-known Sonnet 116 'Let me not to the Marriage of True Minds' [recorded], we find there is a certain argumentative thread in the opening, as though Shakespeare was needing to convince himself against all the evidence that perfect love is possible though rare. Otherwise, he says, it is not true love:

> Love is not love
> Which alters when it alteration finds,
> Or bends with the remover to remove:
> O, No!

This is therefore the one thought to dominate all the delivery. In spite of all difficulties, dangers, disasters, the ravages of time, true love will triumph in the end. He finally says, in effect, that this is the truest thing he has ever written, and when one contemplates the vast amount that he did write, this is an immense claim. He further claims that his love is perfect and will therefore by implication withstand all the vicissitudes listed in the sonnet:

> If this be error, and upon me prov'd,
> I never writ, nor no man ever loved.

The couplet is therefore the clinching of the argument, the climax of the matter, and needs to be spoken after a very short pause, which has the effect of:

(1) 'Pointing' climax and giving it emphasis; and
(2) retaining spontaneity, as though the couplet had just that moment been created in the mind.

As with modern sonnets, it is helpful to speak a series of Shakespeare's sonnets as stanzas of a longer poem in order to achieve the compactness of form and regularity of rhythm required. Speakers can lose both rhythm and form in an over-zealous effort to convey meaning, but the three things are interdependent and must grow together in the preparation.

In contrast to the masculine certainty and argumentative thrust of the Shakespeare sonnet is the E. B. Browning 'How do I Love Thee' [recorded] already mentioned. The rhyme scheme here is different. Instead of the ABABCDCDEFEF GG, we have ABBAABBA CDCDCD. This sonnet, therefore, divides itself into octave and sestet in the manner of the Italian, yet its subject-matter flows through to the final line, and this line must be the climax of the speaking.

The meaning presents no difficulty, yet it is often spoken with extreme sadness, which is strange since, though gentle in tone, it is surely also happy. It is the statement of a woman completely surrendering herself to the man even – God willing – to beyond the grave. If we knew nothing of Elizabeth Browning's life, would not the poem itself suggest that the love is returned, though we may equally feel that no man would ever offer quite so complete a surrender in actual fact, even if many have done so in their poems? Indeed, if we read Robert Browning's 'Two in the Campagna', the feeling there is of the inability to share absolutely in another person's every thought and feeling, no matter how close the relationship. But this is perhaps in very general terms the basic difference between the love of a woman for a man and that of a man for a woman. 'I could not love thee dear so well / Loved I not honour more', said Richard Lovelace, and many men will echo this sentiment. We are indeed fortunate to have a wealth of biographical details of the Brownings, and these may help in judging how best to assess the essence of their poetry.

One final sonnet can show a further variety in the form, both in subject-matter and treatment. This is John Donne's 'Death be not Proud' [recorded]. Here the rhyme scheme is ABBAABBACDDC, and the final two lines which are a variation on the rhyme A thus:

> One short sleep past, we wake eternally,
> And death shall be no more: Death thou shalt die!

goes back to the original translations from the Italian made by Wyatt and Surrey in the early sixteenth century. There is the octave, containing the statement of what death is and is not, followed by the sestet which is a list of death's 'failings', leading to the final phrase in which 'death himself' is overthrown. In the speaking, therefore, the sonnet must build up to the eighth line – 'Rest of their bones and soul's delivery' – to which all men go, which is the first climax, and then rebuild itself in the almost contemptuous way in which Donne deals with death as though he were an actual physical adversary to be overcome, as indeed he may well be. The speaker needs the overriding contempt to be there before the sonnet starts, a feeling of complete confidence and superiority which then unfolds itself in a logical and witty way, e.g. the phrase 'Why swellst' thou then?' – before the final *coup de grâce*: 'Death, thou shalt die!' In fact this sonnet is almost an elegant piece of swordsmanship, and this might be an excellent way to approach it.

So this most difficult of forms for the speaker needs concentration on the one idea, appreciation of rhythm, and individual sonnet form, pointing of climax whether at eighth line or in final couplet, and speaking at a speed which will keep the compact shape. There are many ways of listening to poetry, and for some actually to hear the sonnet *form* spoken to perfection is a delight, quite apart from its content. To less accustomed ears it may be the content that gives the delight. Speakers must aim to fulfil both these needs as, of course, one will enhance the other.

The speaking of an ode requires the same deep concentration, but because the ode is longer something of depth must be surrendered and the thinking need not be quite so rapid, though here it must be sustained. John Keats was supreme in this form, and perhaps the simplest and most delightful of all his odes is the 'Ode to Autumn'. The keynote here is warmth, golden fruition, and stillness – everything seems caught in the late heat haze of a perfect autumn day. The only movement in the poem is the 'light wind' in the third stanza which just gently wafts the tiny gnats up and down as it 'lives or dies'. Yet how often this poem sounds mournful in delivery, perhaps due to anticipation of the final line: 'And gathering swallows twitter in the skies.'

One can well imagine Keats wishing to fly to a warmer climate with the swallows, but of all poets he seems the least mournful and melancholy in spite of his poor health and difficult circumstances. Indeed, one of his most endearing traits is his ability to see humour in everything and thereby to preserve a balance in his writing that never descends to self-pity. Even his 'Ode on Melancholy' [recorded] is not in itself at all melancholy. He stresses the fact that life is all light and shade and the 'sadness' of the 'might of melancholy' will only be experienced by those who have also 'burst joy's grape' against their 'palate fine'. The wry smile is also there in stanza two when he says:

> And if thy mistress some rich anger shows,
> Imprison her soft hand, and let her rave,
> And feed deep, deep upon her peerless eyes.

She may be ranting and raving, but she is still beautiful to look upon, and this is surely some compensation for her ill humour.

The first stanza of this poem probably gives the most difficulty to students, since it is a fairly long list of 'tranquillisers', sedatives, and drugs which Keats warns against. A timely warning, indeed, in this day and age. The ten-line stanza needs speaking at a good pace and working up to the climax contained in the last two lines:

> For shade to shade will come too drowsily,
> And drown the wakeful anguish of the soul.

We must be 'awake' to the misery as to the joy. Lists of objects or situations frequently need gathering up fairly swiftly in the speaking or they tend to become portentous and assume too much individual importance instead of being seen as an accumulation of one idea. The structure of this three-stanza ode, therefore, has a brisk opening stanza with an important first climax at the lines shown above; a second stanza which describes the 'melancholy fit' in its first four lines and gives the antidote in the last six, and the final stanza which carries on with the subject of the 'mistress' and makes the point that one day she must die, as joy must die, and as 'aching pleasure' must die. At the very moment when joy is at its height one must instantly be conscious that it cannot last, and this must occasion the sadness which balances the privilege of the experienced joy. This poem is in fact pure Keats, since it embodies not only his philosophy but his own nature which presumably allowed him to have such a philosophy.

The longer 'Ode to the Nightingale' and 'Ode to the Grecian Urn' need immense range and vocal resources to sustain interest and hold concentration. The richness of the language is perfectly matched to the intensity of the thought, and this makes them rewarding study indeed.

Mention of richness of language really pinpoints many of the rewards of speaking and listening to poetry of the past. We are in constant danger of regarding language as functional only. In the highest flights of poetry we apprehend that sound and sense are completely integrated. As T. S. Eliot has pointed out, the music of poetry is not something which exists apart from its meaning, otherwise we could have poetry of musical beauty which makes no sense, and this is not really possible. But we have also to remember Francis Berry, quoted in Chapter 2: 'Language to a poet is not a means to an end, it is the end itself – the language in the constitution of a poem *is* the experience.' If we take a poem like Tennyson's 'Mariana' we see instantly what Francis Berry means. Here the repeated refrain:

> She only said, 'My life is dreary,
>   He cometh not,' she said;
> She said, 'I am aweary, aweary,
>   I would that I were dead!'

with slight variations, ends each stanza. This gives her emotion in sound and sense and saying the words will induce the mood. Similarly, in Tennyson's 'Tithonus', lines like:

> Man comes and tills the field and lies beneath,
> And after many a summer dies the swan.

This not only gives the whole evolution of the seasons, of birth, and of death, but the very feel of those words in the mouth is a sensual thing, which when spoken will pervade the whole body of the speaker, or should do. Lines of this quality are magical in their own right. They ring in the mind even when the total poem may be forgotten. This particular poem extends the speaker in thought as well as in language, since Tennyson evokes an imaginative image of his 'Muse' coming to give him a poem within the framework of the story of the God granted immortality but not eternal youth. When the muse comes and has no poem to impart, we feel the whole weight of grief and desolation which must be suffered by any artist who feels his gift is waning. The terrifying emptiness of life in such circumstances comes through the remarkable language used to describe it (Tennyson's 'Tithonus'):

> Ere yet they blind the stars, and the wild team
> Which love thee, yearning for thy yoke, arise,
> And shake the darkness from their loosen'd manes,
> And beat the twilight into flakes of fire.
>
> Lo! ever thus thou growest beautiful
> In silence, then before thine answer given
> Departest, and thy tears are on my cheek.

Speaking poetry of the past extends the speaker in every direction –
imaginatively, vocally, and sensually. There is no doubt that it exapnds
the horizons of experience by virtue of this extra dimension of unfamiliar
language, which is literally a new sensation. It encourages a greater
breadth of delivery. To speak a line like Shelley's 'Swiftly walk o'er the
western wave, spirit of night' from 'To Night' necessitates a slight holding
of the vowel sounds to give the sweep of the imaginative sense of the line,
something which a more clipped colloquial delivery could never achieve.
But again it must be stressed that this is the imaginative *sense* insisting on a
delivery which synchronises with thought, not an imposed speech sound
unsupported by true imaginative thinking. Shelley is a much more
sinewy poet than many speakers seem to realise, and far more masculine.
For instance, 'Invocation', where the Spirit of Delight is addressed as a
person, challengingly and forcefully, and chided for being so often absent.
How often is the word 'delight' allowed to colour the whole speaking,
whereas it is the very absence of delight of which Shelley is complaining,
a situation which would seem to call for a rather disgruntled tone of voice,
not a caressingly lyrical one. Unlike Keats, Shelley did suffer from a high
degree of self-pity and does lack humour, but the strength and structure
in, for example, 'Lines written in dejection near Naples' are very comparable to a speaker with 'Ode to a Nightingale', and can be equally
rewarding.

Too often it seems that these great voices from the past are dismissed by
modern speakers as being too hackneyed for fresh interpretation or too
rich in language for modern ears. But once their use of language has been
acquired by the speaker as a natural expression, and he can then go on to
find the essence of the actual poems, and discover thereby how closely it
mirrors the experiences and difficulties of his own generation, then the
listeners receive a true experience couched in magnificent language, which
will release them into new areas of sound/sense consciousness.

The lyrics of major and minor poets alike have frequently been a
source of inspiration to musicians, sometimes happily, sometimes not so.
Generally speaking, the more complete a poem is in itself, the less it appears
to take kindly to a musical setting. The main problem for the musician is

to select a musical rhythm which does not work against the natural speech rhythm and therefore the sense of the poem. Where the musician is also the poet, as in the case of, for example, Thomas Campion in the sixteenth century or Ivor Gurney in the twentieth, then the successful marriage is assured. In our own time Benjamin Britten has been supreme in finding exactly the right lyric to set, and producing most sensitive frameworks, e.g. Blake's 'O Rose thou art Sick', Tennyson's 'The Splendour Falls', or Keats's 'Sonnet to Sleep'. The war poems of Wilfred Owen, however, seem to this one ear quite unsuited to musical addition, but this is perhaps a too personal criticism. Sometimes knowledge of the musical setting is a great disadvantage to a speaker, who cannot quite divorce poem from setting, with the result that the voice moves uncertainly between musical and speech tunes. Certainly too intimate knowledge of a poem's speaking qualities makes it more difficult to accept it happily in another medium. Christina Rossetti's 'Remember Me' – a most poignant sonnet – was recently recorded set to modern music and, though sung most sensitively, the two periods seemed very much at odds with one another, and the poem's stature reduced. On the other hand, the Stanford setting of Keats's 'La Belle Dame Sans Merci' adds considerably to the dramatic quality and eerie atmosphere of the original poem.

As always, Shakespeare transcends all argument, and his songs seem equally happy with or without music. Knowledge of the standard tunes still leaves the words of 'Full Fathom Five', 'Orpheus with his Lute', or even 'O Mistress Mine' eminently speakable, while the 'Dirge' [recorded] from *Cymbeline* offers equal scope to singer or speaker. Sometimes in the context of the play it can sound very doleful indeed, yet the words are anything but. Shakespeare is here making a tremendous comment on death. He is making the important point that death takes us out of the reach of all mortal ills:

> Fear no more the lightning flash
>   Nor the all-dread thunder stone;
> Fear not slander, censure rash;
>   Thou hast finished joy and moan:

There is no more to dread and all is peace. The same 'message' in fact as

Edward Thomas's 'without pleasure, without pain / On the dead oak tree bough'. Therefore the speaking and/or the musical setting will underline this quiet mood of triumph and the certainty of a peace 'which passeth all understanding'.

Truly it has been said that it profit a man little to have read all the masterpieces of the arts or philosophies of the world if it has no effect on his sensibility or his behaviour. One final lyric poem from the seventeenth century will demonstrate the power of poetry to modify one's sensibilities – the poem 'The Salutation' by Thomas Traherne [recorded]. Here the poet makes us realise the gift of life. He sees every day as though through the eyes of a newly born child.

> These little limbs,
> These eyes and hands which here I find,
> This panting heart wherewith my life begins;
> Where have ye been? Behind
> What curtain were ye from me hid so long!
> Where was, in what abyss, my new-made tongue?

Throughout the six stanzas all the glories of the world and of the five senses are slowly contemplated with growing wonder and amazement at the good fortune in finding oneself an occupant of such a treasure house, from being 'beneath the dust' in a 'chaos' to having:

> Such sounds to hear, such hands to feel, such feet,
> Such eyes and objects, on the ground to meet.

Of all these things, life itself is the most precious:

> Such sacred treasures are the limbs of boys
> In which a soul doth dwell:
> Their organised joints and azure veins
> More wealth include than the dead World contains.

And all these glories are there for the taking, free, *gratis*, and for nothing – a gift from God:

> But that they mine should be who nothing was,
> That strangest is of all; yet brought to pass.

Once again the greatest and deepest emotions produce the least vocal movement. If this poem is felt, it can be spoken, and no one who speaks it and believes it will ever feel quite the same again.

On the subject of narrative verse, Vernon Scannell, in 'Letter to a Poet', says:

> The novelist, resourceful spiv,
> Has robbed us of the narrative,

and good up-to-date narratives can be hard to find. But this is one of the oldest and most popular forms of poetry, from such famous nineteenth-century narratives as Coleridge's 'Rime of the Ancient Mariner', Tennyson's 'Lady of Shalott', Byron's 'Don Juan', and so on, back to the unknown authors of the metrical narrative, rhymed romances, and historical songs which flourished between the twelfth and seventeenth centuries. The ballad was particularly alive in the fifteenth century though it began long before and continued long after. Its direct story-line and simple metrical form make it ideal for word-of-mouth communication, and it is therefore excellent for students of verse-speaking. Teachers and actors frequently possess a gift for story-telling and can hold their listeners enthralled in verse with a strong narrative thread. Longer narratives can be introduced in a 'serial' form, with episodes arranged to sustain interest.

In this type of reading it is, of course, the story-line which will dominate. Language, form, rhythm, and character all support this. In the well-known 'Canterbury Tales' of Chaucer, character dominates narrative, and while the portraits are painted in entire simplicity, each member of the group stands out distinctly, so that he or she remains not only an individual, but a recognisable type, as true today as then, a gift Chaucer shares with Shakespeare. This accurate character drawing contrasts sharply with the personifications of vices and virtues which exist in the allegorical narratives like Spenser's 'Faerie Queene' – somewhat rich in sustained lyricism for modern ears.

Epics such as Milton's 'Paradise Lost' are distinguished for their sustained dignity of style, and require grandeur of delivery to match their lofty subject-matter. But passages from epic poetry can be tremendously colourful and dramatic, and offer a great challenge to speakers with vitality and wide vocal range.

The nineteenth-century narratives are widely varied in both tone and intent. Frequently the poet is as it were 'narrator', and the speaker needs to characterise the poet as much as his imagined people. For example, Byron's 'Don Juan'. Here it is not Don Juan we present but Byron himself. He tantalisingly drops little bits of narrative, then stands aside to comment on the situation, and this must be made clear in the reading, and enables quite long passages to be sustained without effort since there is this constant contrast in tone of voice. Coleridge was able to evoke dramatic fantasy out of very simple language in the 'Ancient Mariner', but Wordsworth in, for example, 'Resolution and Independence' or 'Michael' tends to fall into terrible traps of rhyming, and this makes him less satisfactory to a speaker as a narrative poet. He is, of course, much more rewarding in his autobiographical work, and selections from 'Tintern Abbey', 'The Prelude', or 'The Excursion' offer personal narrative of rare quality which it is a privilege to speak. Tennyson's poetry is mainly memorable for its lyrical quality, but his language is used to the service of the narrative in such poems as 'Mariana' or 'Tithonus' already quoted. A story is there for the speaker to communicate even if in both cases it is a fairly static one. Like Wordsworth, his most moving poem is his record of personal feeling, the retracing of his happy association with Arthur Hallam in 'In Memoriam', while Robert Browning's long narrative 'The Ring and the Book' illustrates how various are the different views different people take of a single situation.

Summarising narrative speaking, it is as always the thought which leads the speech, but here it is not an emotion as in a sonnet, lyric, or ode, but a story. The pace will vary with the action, the pitch with the mood or character; there will be use of pause to allow episodes to modulate and situations to change; the voice will be coloured by the colour of the descriptive passages where they occur; there can be use of helpful gesture or movement, and certainly position of head and facial expression will emphasise the tale being told. As has already been said, this need for concentration on a story is an excellent start to the more difficult art of concentrating on a poet and his intimate moods, and all audiences enjoy and appreciate a tale well told.

The greatest wealth of dramatic poetry of the past lies in the drama, and the overriding form is blank verse – the unrhymed iambic pentameter which formed the basis of the plays of the great dramatists of the Elizabethan and Jacobean periods. This speaking must include all the arts of characterisation which are outside the scope of this book. Passages taken out of context are never really satisfactory since they do not fulfil the poet's intention, which was to present a complete play. But where the complete play was not satisfactory there may well be magnificent pieces of blank verse which are complete in themselves. For example, the unfinished *Death's Jest Book* which broke the heart and the health of its creator Thomas Lovell Beddoes. The play is an uneasy mixture of *Othello*, *The Tempest*, and *Hamlet*, yet some fine speeches are given to its central characters, and the play contains philosophies which are not dependent on plot. Beddoes made copious revisions, and in one of these Sibylla, on the death of her lover Wolfram, makes a plea for a healthier attitude towards death. In splendid and dramatic language [recorded] she points out that:

> Belief in death is the fell superstition,
> That hath appalled mankind and chained it down,
> A slave unto the dismal mystery
> Which old opinion dreams beneath the tombstone.

She maintains that the body is a mere part of the whole:

> Aye this is cold, that was a glance of him
> Out of the depth of his immortal self;
> This utterance and token of his being
> His spirit hath let fall, and now is gone
> To fill up nature and complete her being.

What need therefore for sorrow:

> Say not he's dead –
> The word is vile – but that he is henceforth
> No more excepted from eternity.

Blank verse is not difficult to speak since the metre most natural to the English language is undoubtedly the iambic. In the hands of a master poet it is a most flexible instrument, capable of many variations and diversities. This speech and others like it need the personality of the character speaking them, and therefore they offer a new challenge to the verse speaker whose art now becomes that of the actor. Some of the dramatic poems of Browning also need this assumption of character, e.g. 'My Last Duchess', 'Porphyria's Lover', 'A Toccata of Galuppi's', although in 'Two in the Campagna' it is once again the poet himself we seek.

So to humorous, satiric, and didactic verse. Many of the finest examples of satire are no longer of interest except to the English specialist or the historian, since their subject-matter was too tied to their own time, e.g. Samuel Butler's 'Hudibras' (against the Presbyterians); Dryden's 'The Hind and the Panther' (against the churches of Rome and England) or his 'Absolom and Achitophel' (against the Whigs). But there is one voice in this field which transcends period – that of Alexander Pope, since much of his subject-matter was, like Shakespeare's, 'not of an age but for all time'. In his later life he turned almost entirely to satire, and it was then that he wrote the 'Dunciad' which castigated bad poets, the 'Moral Essays', and the 'Imitations of Horace', all of which can yield excellent passages for speaking. Finally, he set out to present a complete philosophy for mankind in his 'Essay on Man'. If we take one passage from Epistle 1, this will serve as an example for all didactic speaking of this kind.

In lyric verse it is the emotion, in narrative verse the story, in dramatic verse the character which predominates. In much of Pope's verse it is the satire, but in 'Essay on Man' it is the argument. Every vocal device must be employed to make the points clear, and something of the character of Pope himself seems necessary – an acid quality which would surely have been betrayed in eyes and tightness of mouth. Physical deformity must be hard to bear. The majority of saints have been beautiful, or perhaps have only appeared so. At any rate Pope was no saint, and whilst he must be read in a manner comprehensible and acceptable to this generation, he must not sound like John Wesley. There is some contempt even in the first two words of the chosen passage, which begins;

> Presumptuous man! the reason wouldst thou find, [Recorded]
> Why formed so weak, so little and so blind?

The couplets with their end-of-line rhymes are going to become very
monotonous if the speech tune is allowed to repeat itself, so every chance
must be taken to vary tone and tune. As the second line poses a question,
the voice is left on an upward inflection. The next two lines give opportunity for lowered pitch – almost as a sort of undertone:

> First, if thou canst, the harder reason guess,
> Why formed no weaker, blinder, and no less

'Less', of course, is the climax and therefore the operative word. Now
Pope gives a list of areas of inquiry:

> Ask of thy mother earth, why oaks are made
> Taller and stronger than the weeds they shade?
> Or ask of yonder argent fields above,
> Why Jove's satellites are less than Jove?

Again this 'list' needs building up to the climax word 'Jove' – and there
has to be a small pause after the first mention of 'Jove', to take the place
of the one unstressed syllable otherwise missing from the line. The enjambment at 'oaks are made' needs the suspensory pause to carry over the
sense. Again the voice has been left 'in the air' on the question. Now it
falls again to build to the next climax, which occurs on yet a third question:

> And all the question, (wrangle e'er so long)
> Is only this, if God has placed him wrong?

The words in parentheses are, as always, spoken on a slightly lower pitch,
since they intrude on the flow of sense, and the 'question' is in this case a
rhetorical one so the voice is not left on an upward inflection and the
speech tune is therefore varied on the listener's ear. Care must now be
taken that the words necessary to the argument are given emphasis, and
that the emphasis itself is varied. Sometimes the use of stress or extra weight
is adequate:

> In *human* works, though laboured on with pain,   [*stress*]
> A thousand movements scarce one purpose gain;
> In God's (pause) one *single* can its end produce,   [*stress*]
> Yet serves to second too, some *other* use.   [*inflection*]

Emphasis therefore is twice made by stress, once by pause, and once by inflection. Inflection is the voice moving very slightly and smoothly through a swift series of notes either upwards, downwards, or both, the infinitesimal movement drawing gentle attention to the word thus inflected. This is a more subtle use of emphasis than stress since it is more delicate and less weighty. It must be noted, too, that rhymed words are always a means of emphasis, which is why they are used, and they generally need no other assistance. The very fact that they rhyme offers an echo to the listener which draws attention to the rhyming words. For example, in the next four lines:

> So *Man*, who here seems principal alone,   [*lower pitch for parentheses*]
> Perhaps acts second to some sphere unknown,
> Touches some wheel, or verges to some goal;
> 'Tis but a *part* we see, and not a whole.

In this passage it would seem a good idea to draw attention to 'Man' as opposed to 'God' by inflecting the voice on this word and to give extra weight to the word 'part' by stress, but 'whole' because it rhymes with 'goal' needs less attention.

By this it will be seen that to sustain interest in the very regular rhythm and rhyme it is necessary to use the voice persuasively to urge the listeners to follow the argument. One is conscious of caressing certain words with loving care – spitting out others, sharpening up all the consonants to 'point' the force of reason, indicating by gesture or head movement where it seems helpful, pausing tellingly to let a point sink in or gathering up several to a climax, in fact being in complete mental and vocal control of the subject-matter and concentrating entirely on communicating this to the listeners. Sometimes volume can be increased or decreased – a soft note in the voice can be as effective as a shouted one – and certainly within the overall rhythm there must be many varieties of pace. Importance of matter will govern these changes. If the matter is of paramount importance, then it takes a slightly slower pace. If more trivial, it can be gathered up and tossed off lightly, an extension of the 'throw away' technique discussed in the previous chapter.

To start beginners or young speakers with such material would obviously not be wise, since a high degree of artifice is essential, though even here the poet's intention is all, and the speaker's mind concentrates entirely on putting over his 'message'. But his voice is consciously used to the poet's service, and this must occasion some degree of self-consciousness which could be unfortunate in a student. In some of Pope's pure satires there is more venom but also more humour, and as in all humorous verse, though the points are appreciated by the speaker, they must be presented to the listeners with high seriousness or they will fail to amuse. It is the contrast between the seriousness of the outward appearance of the matter and the knowledge of inner humour of the situation that makes the comedy. Example from 'The Rape of the Lock':

> Resolved to win, he meditates the way,
> By force to ravish, or by fraud betray;
> For when success a lover's toils attends,
> Few ask if fraud or force attain'd his ends.

Dissecting material in this way can never be satisfactory, but it may help aspiring speakers to see the possibilities, and then personal experiment can develop individual style. Style itself is, after all, a matter of individuality. It is the way in which each individual speaker tackles the problems which gives such a wide range of interpretations, all of which – if sincerely presented – can add to our knowledge of both poet and poetry.

No book on the speaking of poetry can entirely ignore the highly complex verse of the man who has been called the father of modern poetry, Gerard Manley Hopkins, since he must be one of the most difficult poets to speak with even partial success. Hopkins explored early English poetry to find a revised rhythmic structure which might revitalise poetry by the vigour of a more primitive people. The result was a highly individual style of writing to match a highly individual thought. He himself wrote copious notes on his created 'sprung' and 'counterpointed' rhythms and on his experiments with language, and reading all that he had to say will help the speaker to understand his mystical world of intense feeling, intimate vision, and ultimate verbal expression. But rhythm, whether 'sprung' or 'natural', is a difficult subject to write about or talk about; it is has to be experienced. Richards in his book *Principles of Literary Criticism*, says;

Rhythm, and its specialised form Metre, depend upon repetition and expectancy.

Metre, for the most difficult and most delicate utterances is the all but inevitable means.

In Hopkins much of the difficulty for both speaker and listener is the unexpectancy of both rhythm and metre. He needed to discover for himself complicated rhythms and patterns to express his complex thought, and the speaker will have to trace his way back to the poet's thought here as elsewhere, and the thought is as complex as the rhythms chosen to express it.

But there is also the problem of entering as fully as he did into the subject-matter. In one of the more simple sonnets, e.g. 'The Sea and the Skylark', the actual sound, feel, motion, sensation, mood of the sea itself is evoked by:

> the tide that ramps against the shore;
> With a flood or a fall, low lull-off or all roar,
> Frequenting there while moon shall wear and wend.

The word 'ramps' when spoken gives the sensation that the sea itself must feel as it hits the land. One becomes the sea. One does not stand outside describing it. Similarly with the sound of the lark's song:

> His rash-fresh re-winded new skeinèd score
> In crisps of curl off wild winch whirl, and pour
> And pelt music, till none's to spill nor spend.

The sound is experienced, drawn, and painted on the air, bubbles up in the throat and spills over, and the bird's exhaustion after song is actually felt by the poet. So you are first of all standing listening to the sound of the sea and the skylark. Then you are experiencing the being of the sea, the being of the bird, and the final exhaustion of the bird, before the last six lines of the poem give the poet's summing up of their purity compared with man's 'slime'. Truly this goes beyond the speaking of poetry to the inhabiting of poetry, as Hopkins went beyond the ranges of normal thought processes in his search for the inner life of things. It is doubtful whether all of his significances can be expressed in the spoken word, though he himself was always anxious for his poetry to be heard.

But even if all cannot be conveyed, much can be attempted, especially in the simpler poems such as the one quoted. The main thing is to keep the strength which informs the lyricisim always dominant. Spoken this way the poems can give much to a perceptive listener. What is not so acceptable is the delight in mere sound which some speakers of Hopkins manifest, without really experiencing his delight in the reason for the sound, or his despair either (from 'Pied Beauty').

> Fresh-firecoal chestnut falls; finches wings;
> Landscape plotted and pieced – fold, fallow and plough;
> And all trades, their gear and tackle and trim.

This can easily be made to sound like a description of a pretty water-colour picture instead of earth, trees, leather, metal, etc. Indeed, it can sound like Herrick and not Hopkins, who, like Shelley, suffers greatly from being reduced in weight by speakers who once again see the surface of the poems rather than their core. There is an iron hand inside each velvet glove.

One final point: once sufficient control of breath has been acquired to speak with ease the compound words and phrases, then the main imaginative problem is that of holding the thread of thought steady and constant and stretching it to cover the alliterative sequences without becoming word or self-conscious, e.g. 'The Leaden Echo':

> Ruck and wrinkle, drooping, dying, death's worst, winding
> sheets, tombs and worms and tumbling to decay;
> So be beginning, be beginning to despair.
> O there's none; no no no there's none:
> Be beginning to despair, to despair,
> Despair, despair, despair, despair.

But we cannot leave the subject at such a low ebb! In 'The Golden Echo' Hopkins gives us hope:

> There is one, yes I have one (Hush there!)
> Only not within seeing of the sun,
> Not within the singeing of the strong sun,
> Tall sun's tingeing, or treacherous the tainting of the earth's air,
> Somewhere elsewhere there is ah well where! one,
> One.

CHAPTER 7

Interpretation III: Poetry of the Future

Poetry and Jazz

I see brains and lips closed, tympans and temples unstruck,
Until that comes which has the quality to strike and to unclose,
Until that comes which has the quality to bring forth what lies slumbering
    forever ready in all words.

(WALT WHITMAN, 'Vocalism'.)

In his perceptive and fascinating book *Language and Silence*, George
Steiner refers to the fact that culture is not automatically a humanising
force. He asks: 'Does some great boredom and surfeit of abstraction grow
up inside literate civilisation preparing it for the release of barbarism?'

In greatly simplified terms, might not this have been caused by non-
participation in the humanising effects of the arts, by the removal of the
active therapeutic involvement to the passive response only? Might not
the phenomena of pop culture viewed with such mistrust by the older
generation be a healthy sign of a return to personal involvement in
theatrical presentation, the beginnings of 'total theatre'? Certainly this
trend has also begun in the teaching of school drama, which now becomes
more a personal exploration than the exploiting of a talent. In general,
education classes are becoming far nearer to discussion groups, with the
teacher as group leader, rather than a dictation of facts to be taken down
and memorised.

In the legitimate theatre there is much concern with arena presentation,
theatre-in-the-round, and removal of proscenium arch, front curtain, and
so on. Developments through Brechtian Theatre and Artaud's Theatre of
Cruelty, the Theatre of the Absurd, and Peter Brook's experiments in

total theatre and revival of primitive religious ritual, all reflect a desire to remove barriers between players and playgoers and to involve the audience much more in what is taking place.

Obviously no one can be personally involved in all the arts, and some may have no facility in any of them; but might it not be possible that the actual wielding of a paintbrush, however inadequately, teaches more about the art of painting than all the passive gazing at world masterpieces, however well informed the gazer may be? Education does its best. Practically all schools encourage individual participation in improvisation and in modern dance sessions, in pottery and in painting, in the playing of some musical instrument, and in the writing of poetry. But against this healthy sign must be put the vast commercial interests in recording and in television which tend to encourage passive rather than active involvement. The enormous popularity of modern as well as more traditional 'folk' music reveals the need for self-identification and audience participation, and poetry and jazz is an extension of this need. The enthusiasm it arouses in schools, colleges, and universities where it has been presented is always in the realm of 'this is something *we* could do', and while standards of success will vary widely, this is surely a very healthy response and comes in the field of true education. Some of the excellent questions asked after performances may be answered in this chapter, and while no one can really foresee the poetry of the future, there is little doubt that poetry and jazz is here to stay. The poets who take part in these programmes are becoming more and more enthusiastic, and here they are meeting their audiences face to face, not in the rather rarified atmosphere of the old-styled 'poetry readings' but in the stimulating and exciting atmosphere of modern jazz.

One of the first questions to be asked by students when contemplating their own programmes is what music, what poems, and how do we go about promoting the 'marriage' ceremony? Before offering my own contribution it seems right to hear from a musician and a poet, both of whom have been outstandingly successful in writing original poetry and music in collaboration, and whose work reveals a growing mastery over what is virtually a new medium. First the musician – Michael Garrick, pianist and composer, who has been with poetry and jazz since its inception at Hampstead Town Hall in 1961 in collaboration with the poet Jeremy Robson, himself a jazz enthusiast. Michael Garrick, apart from being a superb pianist, holds an honours degree in English and therefore is in a unique position to see the possibilities in both arts. He has set poems by, amongst others, Adrian Mitchell, Thomas Blackburn, Vernon Scannell, Jeremy Robson, and Douglas Hill, but nowhere has his collaboration with a poet been more fruitful than with John Smith, whose 'Five Songs of Resurrection' and 'Four Ritual Dances', together with other jazz poems which he will himself discuss, have been written especially for jazz and have set a new standard for others to match. From an article which first appeared in the *Poetry Review*, here are Michael Garrick's views on poetry and jazz.

'My original justification of poetry and jazz was a social one: people who love jazz and normally hate poetry are learning something new: people who love poetry only begin to feel that there's "something in jazz" after all. So that in one audience, two cultures mix and learn to love each other. We ourselves never first of all bothered to work out *why* we were doing it: as far as we were concerned it was enjoyable. But one must, I suppose, in a critical world, have a rationale ready, so here goes.

'Poetry is musical speech and jazz articulate musical sound. They are really two sides of the same thing: the poet sings the truth about the world as revealed to him in his individuality: the musician speaks of love and pain according to *his* vision. We arrive at a unity of experience because we have a presentation of the world from two sides which must of necessity be complementary, not contradictory, if the artists are good ones. Man is many-sided: those who think that the poetry detracts from the jazz or vice versa have, as Laurie Lee puts it, "one-beat minds".

'Both are aural forms but their appeal catches a man in different places. Poetry mostly reaches the heart via the head: jazz rises to the heart via the belly. The whole man is involved. When neither jazz nor poetry reach their true objective which is the heart then you have the common travesties of our times – a hi-fi intellectualism on the one hand or the modern fashion of muck-paddling on the other, both of them essentially isolationist forms of self-indulgence.

'In preparing music for a particular poem, the poem – being a precise expression in words – determines the emotional mood which the music may then help to explore. Musical phrases, being far more ambiguous and thus more universal than verbal ones, work in the realm of un-intellectualised feeling, where nothing is as yet defined as a specific idea. To these the poet brings thought and lifts the feeling into verbal consciousness, illuminating – and limiting them. Poetry is born. The jazz remains a common pool of human feeling out of which the poet has drawn his own particularised, verbal expression which is then complementary to it.

'Poetry in juxtaposition, as well as combined with jazz, succeeds I think because human needs are rhythmic. One longs for the precise, the definite, and then by turns for that with which one can relax because the demand on verbal thinking is removed.

'There is also this. We have forgotten that poetry is a public art. People have always loved prophets. It is in this role that a poet inevitably appears in an auditorium: after all, we have all come to honour him and hear his wise words. He should live up to it. When he does, we have a powerful high priest indeed – but not until he has hold of the vitals of his recipients. That is where the jazz comes in (and indeed should never have been left out, but you know what civilisation is).

'Today we all long for a return of ceremonial magic, from which we have been divorced for so many centuries. "Art forms" change continually but the purpose of art – that of bringing man into closer contact with his true nature and the forces which sustain him – remains much the same. And the purpose of ritual magic (which has become obscure) was never any different either. So our way ahead is fairly clear. Most entertainment is far too carefully "angled" to achieve this. If we've proved nothing else we have shown that people are not quite so categorised as many promoters assume.

'That this is so is indicated by the unanimous surprise and delight expressed by the poets themselves when they find a warmth of response from poetry and jazz audiences which they had given up long ago like a search for the Holy Grail. "These shows are so full of life compared to ordinary poetry readings."

'I feel that poetry and jazz will develop in scope as time goes on. It is true, however, that some things are possible in one decade which slip away from one in the next, and those things which are self-consciously "new" are notoriously prone to this.

'Everything depends on the speed with which we loosen our categories and undermine the fortresses of specialisation. A modern intelligence should be capable of seeing further than the circumference of its own particular (albeit brilliantly lit) arena. Maybe if the light were not so overbearingly bright it would be easier to see what romps and scampers about outside.

'Obviously the jazz mood is not for the discursive, the philosophic poem. But it has its place with what is direct and emotive. It seems to work best with the narrative, the lyric and the mantric. One of the best jazz poems I have ever encountered was not specifically written for jazz, but it "sets" perfectly to the traditional 12-bar blues sequence. It is called "The Fruit is Swinging" – it was written by John A. Harvey, and it is now a signature tune for the concerts we give with Betty Mulcahy:

> Garden of Eden,
> Flower of Man's beginning,
> Man's undoing,
> Dwelt one,
> Adam,
> Who breathed
> The Breath of Life
> and with him
> Eve, his solace.
> > But,
> In that Garden's beauty
> A Devil appeared,
> A Devil snake,
> To tempt sweet Eve.

Pluck the Fruit of Life's Beginning,
Take the Fruit of Life and taste its sweet;
O take no heed of Adam as he rests in yonder shadow,
The Fruit is swinging!
                              It hangs not high!
It hangs not high up on the bough!
For Eve the Fruit is swinging!
When you have eaten,
Then all Knowledge from the Tree of Life
Will be yours, O Eve, to hold
For EVER and for Ever and for ever – –
                              AMEN!

What a pity, as you sit here reading, that you don't hear the music too!'

And here are the poet's views expressed by John Smith:

'My first introduction to the world of poetry and jazz, in so far as it concerned my own work, was when Michael Garrick played over to me the setting he had composed for an already published poem of mine entitled "A True Story":

My eldest uncle had an extraordinary habit
Of turning young girls into birds;
He kept them in exquisitely jewelled cages.
How he did it I could not tell,
But only that they were inexplicably beautiful.

He was an elegant gentleman of fifty-six
And lived in a Georgian terrace house in Town
Surrounded by his captives' sumptuous, delicate plumage.
They were rarer than nightingales he used to say
And indeed I suppose they undoubtedly were in their way.

Mostly these girls were 'orphans' or 'actresses'
And so they were seldom missed.
They longed in their dreams to be beautiful and admired,
Or so my uncle said with his faint Edwardian smile,
Though I thought I detected a certain trace of guile.

Of course no one knew but me of his strange passion,
Till one day a careless old fool of a cleaner left
Unlatched to the air the door of a gold prison
And out through an open window a mauve bird flew
Like an angel descending to earth for a god's-eye view.

Alas my uncle never recovered his poise.
He roamed the unholy streets six months without pause.
His family were shocked and I alone understood
And wept, when after a night of fantastic alarms
He was found in a park, a naked dead girl in his arms.

'The poem itself, though it has I hope psychological depth and certainly a disturbing conclusion, has an elegant, slightly sardonic and deliberately period surface and I was at once delighted by the way in which by the skilful use of Mozartian pastiche, Michael Garrick had pointed up some of these features. The combination of the two elements, to judge from the audience response, seems to have been successful. I have since then heard many poems "set" to music by this same composer and have found the combination of the spoken word against a musical structure very effective. There is nothing startlingly new in this combination – except in so far as the musical element is "jazz" rather than "classical", for experiments of this kind have often been made ranging from Berlioz's *Lelio*, through Schoenberg's *Pierrot Lunaire* (though in that seminal work it is speech-song that is used), Debussy's *Martyrdom of St. Sebastian*, Edith Sitwell's *Facade* with music by Walton, to the many combinations of poets and musicians in recent years here and particularly in America. Successful as many of these settings are I wanted something slightly different. Apart from the poem "A True Story", all my subsequent poems spoken to Jazz have been conceived especially for the medium and for the music of Michael Garrick.

'Superficially, I think it is easy to suppose that the lyrics I have composed for this medium do not differ from my orthodox lyrics, but I hope that a closer examination will show that there is a considerable difference, though it may be difficult to demonstrate exactly what the difference is. Perhaps first of all it might be interesting to comment on the way in which the jazz poems come into being. Many people ask "which comes first, the poem or the music?" and the answer is that with very rare exceptions it is the poem that is the genesis of the work. I propose to take three poems which exhibit attempts to solve different problems that arise when confronted with writing with music in mind – writing poems for jazz, which is different from writing a libretto for an

opera or indeed a lyric for a song. The first necessity is some pre-
conceived idea of how the music is going to sound – what instrument or
combination of instruments will accompany the voice.

'The first group of jazz poems I wrote for Michael Garrick, "Jazz for
Five", was conceived specifically for the instruments of his quintet. The
first poem is pure and in some sense "cold" and tries to mirror certain
qualities of the piano; the second is a sultry, more relaxed love poem
for the bass player; the third is a quick, sharp and finally dramatic poem
for the drums, the fifth a glittering optimistic poem for the trumpet. In
most of these poems there is also a backing by the rest of the quintet. It is
the fourth poem that I would like to look at now. This is a poem conceived for the alto saxophone, and when written was especially related
to the playing of Joe Harriott who has a quality which is both frenetic and
full of tragic undertones. The poem is written as a dialogue for speaker
and saxophonist. The instrument speaks first, setting the dramatic mood
for the opening line; it is then necessary for the two performers to
catch up each other's pace and intensity as the poem continues.

He ran out Crying

He ran out crying
He ran out crying
He said
Oh my most beautiful dear girl
Oh my most beautiful dear girl
He ran out crying

He said
All the windows, all the windows and doors are crying
The locks broken on their hinges are crying
He ran out
Oh my most beautiful
He ran out crying

The air
The air is on fire
And all Christ's tears will not quench it
(He ran out crying)
Where, Oh my most beautiful dear girl,
My most beautiful dear girl lies dying.

'The first noticeable feature is the almost total lack of punctuation and the general fragmentary nature of the poem. The lines are, as it were, a series of individual fragments tied together merely by the urgent pathos of the man suffering loss. This lack of cohesion gives the instrumentalist the freedom to interject his own musical phrases as and when he feels like it; sometimes they are isolated and frame the lines, sometimes they run over, especially at the climax of "the air is on fire". The second obvious feature is the use of repetition and the unsophisticated language. Abstractions are scrupulously avoided and the words are related to actualities. There is no room for speculation; it is a poem in which the emotional impact is paramount.

'An extension of this technique is made in a later poem "Leaping Dance of Death" from a group of four Ritual Dances. These dances are related to the elements and this final poem is obviously a fire dance. It is still conceived within a dramatic framework as is "He ran out Crying", but this time it supposes two figures in opposition: Death, who is playing in a sort of grotesquely mocking and clownish way with a man who is trying to escape. An important distinction between the mood of this poem and the previous one is that here it is *death* that we are concerned with and not dying – two very different things, at least from my point of view.

'The poem was originally planned for a quintet though there is also a version for trio. In performance the verses spoken by death are pointed up by the piano and bass; the man's growing frenzy by the quintet with short solos for trumpet and saxophone between the verses. The rhythm is kept simple but not exact so as to give the voice scope when reading to slur over or bring together certain phrases while keeping the overall rhythm intact. The poem is again very repetitive. A non-jazz poem on this theme would have been, had I written it, far more involved, far more metaphysical, and would have avoided the use of certain clichés which are in the present version because of the necessity of keeping the total effect comprehensible at a first hearing. Here is the poem:

Leaping Dance of Death

I will dance you tight
I will dance you slack
I will dance you crimson
I will dance you black

> *Lay down you dead man*
> *Lay down you gone*
> *Lay down you leaping ghost*
> *Under your stone.*

I will dance you blood
I will dance you mire
I will dance you flesh
And your body on fire

> *Lay down you leaper*
> *Lay down mocking ghost*
> *Lay down you prancing demon*
> *Let me rest.*

I will dance you terror
I will dance you no hope
I will dance you in the air
On a short rope

> *Lay down you leaping ghost*
> *Lay down you nothing*
> *Lay down you twisting fiend*
> *Stop your writhing.*

I will dance you up
And I will dance you down
I will dance you till you dance
In death's nightgown.

> *I will not dance up*
> *In a gown of death*
> *I will not dance down*
> *Out of my level breath*

But I will dance you deaf
And I will dance you dumb
I will dance you danceless
Now, I will dance you
           come!

'The death figure who is confident of the outcome, who knows he is going to win, uses hard simple rhyme sounds and the images that are allowed are all specific and unpleasant; the man on the other hand uses near rhymes, dissonances, until his last verse, and his precision is tempered because he does not know how to name death; he calls him a "nothing", a "leaper", a "gone"; he seems in some ways more wraith-like than death himself, who is hard and actual. The music emphasises this for although the accompaniment to the man's part is more savage it is also more free, mirroring the man's distress, his attempts to escape from the opposing demon; death on the other hand is always accompanied by a phrase which is intentionally banal and extremely hypnotic.

'In the group of poems entitled *Seasons of Love* my intention was to write four poems that could be played on some of the instruments which are at the command of the great jazz player Don Rendell. In "He ran out Crying" the poem is conceived for an isolated voice; in "Leaping Dance of Death" for a quintet or trio in consort; in *Seasons of Love* the instrumentalist is highlighted against the background of the trio consisting of piano, bass and drums. I have tried to match the mood of the poems to the nature of the instruments once again, as in "Jazz for Five", but this time in a more concerted, more strictly lyrical fashion. The first one, which I would like to quote now, is the first of the group, "Song Before Sunrise", written for the flute. What an enchanting instrument the flute is! It has been used by so many composers for lyrical works, never more so perhaps than in Debussy's famous *L'Après-midi d'une Faune*. Of course it has a very wide range of sound and can convey great depths of emotion, but to open this particular jazz suite I wanted the simplest possible sort of spring song, something which would let the flute sing a free open air melody; I wanted innocence but tempered with a little of the pagan nature that perhaps one associates with Pan and Syrinx, for it was Syrinx of course who, when being chased by Pan, was saved from his embraces by being turned by the Gods into a reed – a singing reed.

' "Song Before Sunrise" is quite different from the other two poems I have discussed; it is neither a soliloquy nor a dialogue; it is a lyric

which is to be spoken with the music in much the same way as an early
Elizabethan song might have been sung to music; the words and music
therefore come together; they are performed together, the voice and
the flute doubling the melody. It is lilting and totally "unpretentious",
using images readily comprehensible and the simplest verse structure.

Song Before Sunrise

The girl I loved was as young as April
  The birds flew up and the birds flew down
Her breasts were like the magnolia blossom
  The birds flew up and down

The girl I loved was a willow on a stream
  The fish swam up and the fish swam down
The girl I loved was the light on the water
  The fish swam up and down

The girl I loved was the sky at evening
  The journeying moon sailed up and down
The girl I loved was the quiver of morning
  The moon sailed up and down

And the girl I loved was as beautiful as Time
  The bells rang up and the bells rang down
The bird and the fish and the journeying moon
  And the bells rang up and down
  And the bells rang up and down

'I hope this has some of the weightlessness of a piece of simple em-
broidery. The images are evocative but gentle and are not explained,
the echoes are left as echoes. I have tried to give it a transparent quality
by allowing no development within the subject matter and by choosing
images that are related to freedom but also to impermanence. More
than any other instrument the flute is the instrument of the breath, for
unlike the rest of the woodwind it uses no reeds. The words therefore
are pitched in their weight so as to seem to float on the breath, to be
evanescent and insubstantial.

'Whether in these poems and my other jazz poems I have succeeded in doing what I set out to do it is not for me to say – that is the privilege of the audience or the critic. But I do find the writing for music in this way stimulating and fascinating. The poems I write for jazz are very different, to my mind, from those I write as "straight" poems, which are often more speculative or weighty in subject matter and more complex in structure. I hope that the jazz poems also stand up as poems without the music, in that they show themselves to be fully formed; but they are properly conceived for performance and naturally pose special problems for the speaker of poetry who has to co-operate with a group of musicians in order to build a composite world of sense and sound.'

As both musician and poet have said, jazz poems do not have the 'associated ideas' of the discursive or philosophic poem (see Chapter 4). They need an immediacy and simplicity of meaning if both words and music are to be taken in aurally without undue strain. For the speaker, therefore, the music now takes the place of these associated ideas, guiding and modifying his delivery. The music speaks through him, as do the words – the words making specific what the music suggests. The thought processes of musicians and speaker must be integrated in performance so that the aim is the same. This can be likened to group speaking where individual interpretations are subordinated to the group interpretation, though individuality of expression is retained.

In the first stages of speaking with music there can be a tendency for the speaker to compete with the musicians. This is disastrous since the audience will feel they are being pulled in two different directions, and according to their experience and preference they will either listen to jazz or to words.* With inexperienced speakers the jazz can easily dominate the words, which is just as bad. Therefore the balance between jazz and voice is of paramount importance. The voice has to be amplified by microphone and the microphone used with skill and variety or the speech sound can quickly lose subtlety and become mechanical. In any case, words spoken are generally more significant than words sung, since the sustained

---

* When the two have been conceived together this does not happen, which is why it is to be hoped that more and more poets will attempt this exciting medium.

nature of sung words can dilute meaning. Also the speech rhythms, being different from, though possibly counterpointing, the musical rhythms, will tend to isolate the words to some extent, so that there is never any need for the speaker to force this isolation.

Just as group feeling is built up between the various musicians, each listening and contributing to the others, so between speaker and musicians the same feeling needs to be achieved, so that the listening becomes almost as important as the speaking. One becomes identified with each musician as he takes his solo, and ultimately all is moulded into one's own contribution expressed in words instead of in music. Without this necessary integration, poetry and jazz does not become a truly unified medium.

Because of the improvised nature of true jazz, it requires that the speaker in a poetry and jazz concert be immensely flexible in his own performance. The words will remain the same, but the delivery will vary considerably from performance to performance according to the group mood and the audience's reaction. Michael Garrick has said: 'Jazz is an art of musical improvisation – to match it in verve and spontaneity, cannot poets now begin to free themselves also from the necessity of writing everything down in advance?' This is taking us into the realm of the Welsh Penillion singing where words are improvised by individual singers from a given theme to a fixed melody – the reverse really of poetry and jazz. Improvisation of both words and music might lead to anarchy, and in any case would surely defeat the object, which is to combine a highly disciplined art with a freer one and in doing so to enhance both. Where a poem is 'set' to jazz backing, some people have pointed out that the music ceases to be jazz. But the 'setting' is more of a framework and allows of great variety of treatment from performance to performance, sometimes disconcertingly so for the speaker if he has allowed himself to become too rigid in interpretation.

Thus spontaneity in the speaker is of immense importance and the training discussed in Chapter 4 invaluable. Poet-readers are in a class of their own since they possess the integrity of the creator, but even they are finding the need to 'perform' to some degree since the situation demands it. There is no doubt that speaking to jazz widens the vocal range considerably and releases speakers and poets in a way many would not have thought possible. The speaker must be involved physically as well as mentally and vocally, or his 'performance' can seem over-intellectualised and out of context with his physical situation.

In my own concerts with the Michael Garrick trio, the material is divided into groups exploring the same kind of subject from different points of view, thus enabling us to see things 'in the round'. 'Falling', for example, contains unusual poems on Eve and the Fall of Man, and includes the poem quoted 'The Fruit is Swinging'. 'Casualties' explores death by war; 'Men were Deceivers' is self-explanatory. Whereas other presentations concentrate on poets reading their own work, we use material drawn from a wide range of writers and times, together with jazz music especially prepared to reflect or sustain the moods created by these works. Sometimes we use the words of an old 'standard', i.e. a popular song of the past which has stood the test of time, to create an initial mood for the group, e.g. *Just One of Those Things* or *Who's Sorry Now?*, or a music hall song, e.g. *I do like to be Beside the Seaside* or *If you were the Only Girl in the World*. Sometimes a phrase from a poem which is to be included, e.g. 'A thing of beauty' or 'Remembrance of Things Past'. It is interesting to discover that poems from different periods, like pieces of furniture, can group happily together if chosen for their own intrinsic value. Young people who would not consider attending a straight poetry reading are nevertheless delighted to hear Keats's 'Ode to Autumn' included in a group of poems about the seasons, and Shakespeare's songs and sonnets are, of course, ageless and timeless.

So far we have only discussed in detail poems written by a poet especially for the jazz music of Michael Garrick. But he has also set poems for me to speak which were not designed with music in mind. An interesting one to mention first is 'Prayer Before Birth' by Louis MacNeice since this has already been discussed as a straight poem in Chapter 5. It is treated in this way.

Before the poem begins, the theme, which is based on the phrase 'I am not yet born', appears once by itself, and as the poem begins so a bass solo begins and works up to a climax, drums and piano gradually joining in, on the words 'Let not the man who is beast or who thinks he is God/

Come near me.' After these words the drums have a violent short solo passage. The initial theme now reappears played by the trio, with the voice coming in sadly and despairingly after the first few bars and continuing until the line 'Let them not make me a stone and let them not spill me.'

The music concludes and in the silence that follows the voice says flatly: 'Otherwise kill me.'

Two poems in the group called 'Casualties' have been outstandingly successful. One is an early song by W. H. Auden originally entitled 'Blues', and the other a poem by Archibald MacLeish entitled 'The Young Dead Soldiers'. Auden's poem of despair is spoken on a basic two-beat-in-a-line rhythm against the funereal patter of the drums and a jazz piece by Michael Garrick, already existing in its own right, and called 'Dirge'. That the words and music seem to have been 'made for each other' is one of the minor miracles of this medium. The atmosphere of the poem 'The Young Dead Soldiers', who speak to the living in the quiet of the night and 'when the clock counts', is enhanced by the delicate two-note rhythmic beat of the music which plays quietly behind the words, giving the poignancy of time passing, during which the 'young dead soldiers' feel they are likely to be forgotten.

Other poems which have been set in this way include Wallace Stevens's 'Peter Quince at the Clavier', a poem which specifically mentions music, and in which the jazz backing enhances the sensual nature of the poem, dramatically in 'Eve' by Ralph Hodgson, where the mood of poem and music changes from 'innocence to knowledge', and satirically as background music to a group of poems on the subject of 'Cocktail Party', the music here adding to the cynical sophistication suggested in the words. We have used speaker and piano alone in a gentle satire written by John Smith called 'Secrets',* speaker and drums in a militant poem by Kipling called 'The Vampire', and speaker and bass in a number of folk songs used to set mood and atmosphere at the beginning of a group or as a means of rounding off.

* An exception to the 'words first' rule since here the music of Michael Garrick inspired the words of John Smith (see end of chapter).

There is still much to be discovered. For example, in a group called 'Beside the Seaside' – which starts with the old music hall song – there is an extract from 'Under Milk Wood'. Here bass and voice are used to suggest 'Captain Cat' and piano and voice for 'Rosie Probert', while the drums contribute a soft rhythmic brush stroke reminiscent of the sea. Tribute must here be paid to the highly individual talent of Coleridge Goode on bass, who combines amplified vocal effects with his bowed bass, adding yet another facet of rhythmic sound, and to the inspired and inventive drumming of Colin Barnes and on some occasions Trevor Tomkins. In this way all the individual talents of members of the Garrick trio contribute to the poet's intention.

All this may give some idea of the scope possible in a programme of poetry and jazz which, when presented by myself and the trio, always includes several items of jazz alone and at least one 'straight' poetry item,★ although each individual programme is conceived as an entity and builds to a recognisable climax, rhythmically, emotionally, and intellectually.

This brings me to the one element still missing to my mind from poetry and jazz concerts, namely some use of movement – albeit movement disciplined and completely subordinated to words and music. I have made some tentative excursions into this field in the 'Ritual Dances' since they seem by their very nature to demand some small amount of movement from the speaker. Being myself trained in movement before speech it seems impossible to stand stock-still while saying the words:

> The world sleeps
>   And the world dances;
> The moon recedes,
>   The sun advances;
> All our griefs
>   And all our mirth
> Woke in the making
> Of the earth.

★ Poems of the calibre of 'Sunday Morning' by Wallace Stevens; 'Adam's Dream' by Edwin Muir; 'Orpheus', 'Eurydice', 'Hermes' by Rilke; and 'Mariana' by Tennyson, or selections from 'Don Juan' by Byron, are included as the solo poem, the last proving unsurpassable in wit and mastery of rhyme and astonishingly modern in outlook.

Or in:

> I hold in my left hand water,
>   In my right hand I hold blood;
> I dance the fingers of one hand open
>   To let the rich substance flood.

They are, after all, titled 'Earth Dance of the Body of God' and 'Finger Dance for the Souls of the Drowned', and one stanza from each is enough to show what I mean.

There can be no conclusion to this chapter since the full story of poetry and jazz has yet to be told. Suffice to say that in an atmosphere of relaxation and stimulation young people and older people are listening to the best in poetry from any age combined with jazz music of the highest order. We hope that they too are being inspired to experiment for themselves in this fascinating new medium.

NOTE: Actors in some modern musicals have used a form of 'speaking on pitch' when their singing abilities have been inadequate. Something of this technique is used in poetry and jazz where the two things have been created together, and certainly where words have followed music. This is inevitable since what we may call 'sense or speech tune' will follow musical tune to some extent, and to this same extent the speaker's pitch will adjust. But it is, or should be, still speaking, and not half-singing, and the speaker's voice needs, therefore, to be wide-ranging in pitch in order to make the necessary changes without resorting to song. (See Chapter 4, Part II.)

CHAPTER 8

Preparation of Programmes

For only at last after many years, after chastity, friendship, procreation,
    prudence, and nakedness,
After treading ground and breasting river and lake,
After a loosen'd throat, after absorbing eras, temperaments, races, after
    knowledge, freedom, crimes,
After complete faith, after clarifyings, elevations and removing obstructions,
After these and more, it is just possible there comes to a man, a woman, the
    divine power to speak words;

(WALT WHITMAN, 'Vocalism'.)

In the preparation of his programme the interpreter has his chance of
being something of a creator, and it is one of the most fascinating aspects
of the work. It can be likened to the creative arts since the success of a programme will depend upon the overall shape, the building through a series
of minor climaxes to a final major climax, and the ultimate rounding off.
The shape of any programme is of paramount importance to both speaker
and audience, since this will determine the overall harmony of the work.
As Samuel Beckett says in Martin Esslin's *The Theatre of the Absurd*, 'I am
interested in the shape of ideas even if I don't believe in them. . . . It is the
shape that matters.' Rhythms must be varied yet harmonious and must
modulate easily from one to another or occasionally contrast sharply. The
programme must be unified yet have range and variety of mood, variety
in the length of individual poems and rhythms, and of styles and points of
view. Any programme will reflect the speaker's own personality to some
degree, yet if this factor is allowed to dominate too much the programme
becomes a vehicle for the speaker rather than for the poet or poets whose
words are being used.

123

Because of the relative unpopularity of this subject compared with, say, music, and the modern preference for poets reading their own work, the opportunities for professional work in this field are few. However, there are arts festivals which sponsor poetry readings, there are poetry circles, literary groups, clubs which exist to study the art of the spoken word, and interest is growing all the time. The London Academy of Music and Drama (Tower House, Cromwell Road, SW 5) now have a diploma of verse speaking which gives students opportunities to present a short recital of five items, three to be selected from a given syllabus and two the candidate's own choice, marks being awarded for overall presentation and selection as well as for interpretation, and the Poetry Society (21 Earls Court Square, SW 5) will award a gold medal for excellence at their bi-annual auditions. Several enterprising festivals of music and speech offer a class in which competitors choose a poet, present a written essay on his life and work, and then read in public a selection of his poems with brief commentary. Other organisers might adopt this excellent idea.

Unfortunately the highly competitive nature of some festivals tends to reduce the therapeutic and artistic value of attainment, and criticism is not always entirely constructive or received without rancour. Unlike the now – sadly – defunct English Festival of Spoken Poetry,* there is perhaps too much insistence still on individual voice and speech at the expense of overall interpretation of poem. It is sad, indeed, to hear a sincere and moving piece of speaking criticised for an intrusive *r* or 'glottal shock'. Presumably if these speech faults intrude on the judge's appreciation they must be mentioned, but, it is to be hoped, not given priority, since such things are unlikely to prove distracting to any but a speech specialist, and may well develop self-consciousness in a student speaker. A healthier attitude towards spoken poetry might exist if the judges were poets.

Meanwhile schools can devise their own programmes, guided and

* In the 1920's John and Constance Masefield started a series of verse-speaking festivals which took place in Oxford, and in which professional actors, teachers, and speakers met in an atmosphere which made the contest itself seem of little importance compared with the joy in poetry and poetry speaking. After the war these annual festivals moved to Bedford College, London, still judged always by poets. Owing to financial difficulties they ceased in 1959 and have never been revived.

assisted and sometimes accompanied by their English or speech and drama teacher, who should always be prepared to contribute some speaking of his own. In this art levels of achievement can happily combine in one programme to the benefit of all, and the more attempted the sooner standards will rise and audiences be found.

When spoken poetry takes its rightful place alongside music, it should then be possible to present in public a programme of major poems to discerning listeners without any need for explanation, commentary, or indeed apology. The speaking will be judged on interpretation, the poems having stood the test of time. Thus a programme could merely state, for example:

'Dover Beach'	MATTHEW ARNOLD
'Ode to a Nightingale'	JOHN KEATS
'A Tocatta of Galuppi's'	ROBERT BROWNING
'Tithonus'	LORD TENNYSON
'Rhapsody on a Windy Night'	T. S. ELIOT
'Journey to a War'	Sonnet sequence by W. H. AUDEN.

As with music or song recitals, critics would be invited to comment, and the resulting criticism would read precisely as the criticisms of music taken for granted in daily newspapers. For example: Was the overall rhythm fully sustained? Did the tone convey the mood? Was this or that subtlety sufficiently appreciated and conveyed? Did the phrasing complement the thought?, and so on. A singer or instrumentalist has this opportunity for public hearing and criticism as a professional artist. Why not a speaker? Poems of the calibre of those mentioned should be as well known to the public as are the works of Shakespeare or the music of Beethoven, and individual efforts to realise the poet's intention would be worth striving for and publicly acknowledged.

In the meantime audiences have to be wooed and won over, and every good programme sincerely presented is a step forward; and every bad, shoddily composed, and poorly spoken programme is a step backwards; so the responsibility is great.

As Michael Garrick has said, poetry makes specific what music only suggests, so leaving aside programmes devoted to individual poets, which are, generally speaking, for the specialist rather than for the general public, we have to decide what the programme is to be about and what its intention is. The usual way is to take a theme and explore it in various ways, offering many points of view but not necessarily reaching any exact conclusions, though a general 'summary' and 'rounding off' gives the audience that very necessary feeling of completeness, of 'order out of chaos' mentioned in Chapter 1. Depending on the length of the programme it is desirable to have the subject-matter wide-ranging or there is a danger of using inferior material merely because it fits the theme. It is wise to choose the climax poem early on in order to have a peak or goal for the programme to reach.

Titles in themselves can be fascinating and can suggest deeper aspects of the chosen subject. For example, a programme presented at one of the three-choirs festivals, and involving two readers and one singer, was arranged around the four headings of bible quotations thus:

> In the Beginning. . . .
> The Heavens are telling.
> A sojourner, like all my Fathers. . . .
> A new Heaven and a new Earth.

The scope this offered can easily be imagined. A further programme using musicians had pianist, tenor, soprano, and two readers, and was given in three parts as:

> Birth and Death.
> Light and Dark.
> Old and New.

In this programme speakers and singers shared some poems. For example: Keats's 'La Belle Dame Sans Merci' was spoken and then sung in the Stanford setting; Rupert Brooke's 'Spring Sorrow' was spoken and then sung in the John Ireland setting; and Tennyson's 'Now Sleeps the Crimson Petal' was spoken and then sung in the Roger Quilter setting, thus further linking the two arts.

From George Peele's poem 'What Thing is Love', the title gave a programme for a man and woman ranging from mythology to modern, from the great love stories of the gods to the petty irritations and frustrations of contemporary living. Shakespeare's 'Youth's a stuff . . .' can form the first half of a programme, with 'Will not endure . . .' as the second and concluding half, and 'Black Monday Lovesong', from a poem by A. S. J. Tessimond, gives an opportunity to 'sing the blues' about human relationships.

A programme about the nature of poetry itself developed from one line of a poem by Marianne Moore, in which she states that poetry, if it is to be any good, must present 'Imaginary gardens with real toads in them'.

The title of this programme became 'With Real Toads' and gave the opportunity to present 'poets on poetry' ranging from the sixteenth to the twentieth century.

Where circumstances encourage a visual as well as a vocal expression, and where audiences require to be assisted in their listening, some form of period movement can happily precede poems of the time, the speaker miming the clothes and giving a simple commentary on the social conventions and historical background of each period. Representative music can add greatly to a programme of this nature.

Since the majority of poets have always been keenly sensitive to the world around them a programme devoted to 'The Five Senses' can yield plenty of material and can involve the listeners in an appreciation of their own sensual potentialities. Research will reveal many fine poems under this general heading of which the following are just a few: *Smell* – 'Old Man or Lad's Love' by Edward Thomas; 'Perfumes' by Terence Tiller; 'Flowering Currant' by Eiluned Lewis. *Taste* – 'A Reproof of Gluttony' by Hilaire Belloc; 'In Praise of Old English Roast Beef' by Richard Leveridge; 'A Pipe of Tobacco' by Isaac Browne. *Sound* – 'The Fifth Sense' by Patricia Beer; 'Radio' by A. S. J. Tessimond; 'Cornet Solo' by Cecil Day-Lewis. *Touch* – 'Charles' by Leonard Clark; 'The Carpenter' by Clifford Dyment; 'The Blessing' by James Wright. *Sight* – 'Day' by John Smith; 'Bat' by D. H. Lawrence; 'April Rise' by Laurie Lee.

However, the actual choice of poems must be a personal and individual thing, and the instinct for knowing how best to place them in context comes with practice, trial, and error. It is essential to find the heart of each individual poem or it can well be chosen for its superficial subject-matter and therefore in context with others distorted from its true purpose. Nowhere is this more true than in poems of the senses where one sense may well evoke a poem whose essence then becomes something rather different. For example: 'The Idea of Order at Key West' by Wallace Stevens is occasioned by hearing a girl singing by the sea. But the poem is not about the sense of hearing, as are the three poems already mentioned. It is about order from chaos. Similarly, 'Dover Beach' by Matthew Arnold, though inspired by the sound of the sea, is a poem about human relationships and loss of faith. One could argue that 'Cornet Solo' by C. Day-Lewis and 'Old Man' by Edward Thomas are poems about memory, but in both these poems the sound in the former and the scent in the latter not only cause the mood, but become the mood and therefore the essence of the poem. In 'Dover Beach' and 'The Idea of Order at Key West' the original sound becomes the inspiration for something much deeper and wider in significance, and this could be lost if the poem were placed in the wrong context.

On the other hand, the discreet placing of a poem can help a not-too-knowledgeable audience to see its true purpose. Examination of one complete programme may show this and also show how the programme attempts to fulfil the requirements mentioned at the beginning of the chapter.

The programme was presented as part of a double-bill with Strindberg's *Miss Julie*, and poems were selected which complemented Strindberg's exploration of the biological needs of women. In the play this led Miss Julie into a loveless physical union with her servant, to his contempt and her despair, a despair conditioned in part by the social conventions of the time. The poems chosen and the reason for their selection were as follows: 'Eve' by Ralph Hodgson, because this presents the original innocence and freshness of woman followed by her ultimate knowledge and humiliation, as in the play. 'A Florentine Comedy' by John Smith, inspired by Lucas Cranach's painting of Eve which hangs in the Uffizzi Gallery, the poem showing deep compassion for the whole state of womankind as a result of the sin in the garden. 'Judith of Bethulia' by John Crowe

Ransom, in which the poet deplores the use of her feminine attractions by this biblical character to overthrow and finally to kill Holofernes, the invader of her country. This poem linked also with the preceding one since the statue of Holofernes is mentioned there, and though it is another modern poem it is still concerned with the biblical scene.

The programme has so far presented three strong but fairly short modern poems and the audience should now be ready for something lighter and longer. Too many short poems tax the listener because of the constant need to adjust to various poets and viewpoints, the poem sometimes being all over before the necessary adjustment has been made.

A selection from Byron's long narrative poem 'Don Juan' followed, in which the poet makes the point that:

> There are months which nature grows more merry in,
> March has his hares and May must have his heroine.

This links with the play which is set on Midsummer Eve for the same reason, and the seduction scene from Canto I wherein the beautiful Julia entices the 16-year-old Juan is a further development of woman as the huntress, here described with all Byron's wit and elegance. This was the first 'climax' and the one humorous item.

It was followed by two nineteenth-century poems by women. First a delicate ambiguous little poem by Caroline Norton, 'I do not Love Thee' and then the joyously contained poem by Christina Rossetti, 'A Birthday' – sometimes called by its first line, 'My heart is like a singing bird'. These two poems serve to illustrate a point made in Chapter 6. The Caroline Norton poem tells a poignant little love story in its five four-line stanzas, and seems to demand some knowledge of the author's period, dress, and social conventions in order to build a background for the character which emerges. On the other hand, the Rossetti poem is ageless and timeless – a pure lyric. It requires only appreciation of its emotional content and complete simplicity.

Shakespeare said 'the course of true love never did run smooth', and the Byron narrative is balanced here by the inclusion of Tennyson's 'Mariana' in which the lover does not come. The poem marks the second climax.

W. B. Yeats's poem 'A Last Confession' makes the point that women do not always love equally with mind and body, and he leaves no doubt, through the woman speaking in the poem, which he feels to be the more lasting. This poem is short, strong, and vital, and prepares the way for the reflective 'Dover Beach' by Matthew Arnold which followed. Here the view is widened from the particular to the more general, and this poem gathers up much of what has gone before into the significant line: 'Ah, love, let us be true to one another.'

The final poem in the reading was 'Solomon and the Witch', again by Yeats. This poem returns to the garden of Eden where the programme began and suggests that, although perfection of physical union is an unlikely fact because of the 'brigand apple' and the 'cruelties of choice and chance', we nevertheless spend our lives seeking for it. Yeats says not all the wisdom of Solomon nor all the beauty of Sheba can guarantee success. The final line is a poignant cry: 'O! Solomon! let us try again.'

These poems, though immensely varied in themselves, were none the less all concerned in some way with human relationships and sexual difficulties, the one fulfilled and happy note being the Rossetti poem 'A Birthday'. They were presented with a brief linking commentary,* using a lectern for the Byron, a chair for the narrative poem of Tennyson, some poems being read and some spoken without script, all means of offering variety of visual presentation and giving each poem an individual treatment according to its needs. The whole recital lasted 40 minutes and contained five modern and five nineteenth-century poems, though this last fact was entirely accidental.

It does, however, bring up an important factor often overlooked or misunderstood. Programme planners have to be aware of copyright charges and, with the best will in the world, cannot always include as much modern work as they might wish, because at 7s. 6d., 10s. 6d., or even 12s. 6d. per poem, this is not economically possible. However, if no payment is being received by the speaker and no charge made to the

---

* A commentary can not only put the listeners into the right frame of mind for the next poem, it can also serve to prepare the speaker. Care is needed that explanations are brief and to the point or they can make the poem seem superfluous.

audience, many publishers and poets will allow their work to be used without payment. Nevertheless, permission must be obtained and copyright paid where required, since poets have to make a living like anyone else and cannot be expected to be unpaid script writers to all and sundry.

The programme described was relatively short as it was offered in conjunction with a one-act play, and this might be a good idea for schools or drama societies where those not engaged in the play could develop the play's theme in the way suggested. For example, dramatisation of stories from mythology could be followed by poems dealing with or based upon the same legend, or biblical scenes from medieval mystery plays such as *The Raising of Lazarus* or *The Man Born Blind*; non-communication between individuals, nationalities and/or colours is a favourite topic with modern dramatists, e.g. Adamov, Beckett, Ionesco, and Pinter – all of whom have used the one-act form;* and this subject forms the content of numerous poems. On the subject of youth-in-command, so well explored by William Goldings's *Lord of the Flies*, there is a play called *The Raft* of *the Medusa* by George Kaiser, written for a cast of thirteen teenagers, which might well act as a triggering-off point for poems on the subject, while Brecht seems an obvious choice for both drama and poetry.

Where a poetry reading has to occupy an entire programme of, say, an hour and a half with one interval, the more weighty material will need to be flanked by poems requiring less concentration on the part of the audience, and the subject-matter be much more varied and with more humorous or satirical material included. Sometimes a passage of didactic verse can be examined in detail through the words of other poets writing on the same subject. For example, Pope's lines from 'Imitations of Horace' on the poet's place in society:

> Of little use the man you may suppose,
> Who says in verse what others say in prose;
> Yet let me show a poet's of some weight,
> And (though no soldier) useful to the state.
> What will a child learn sooner than song?

---

* See *The Theatre of the Absurd* by Martin Esslin.

> What better teach a foreigner the tongue?
> What's long or short, each accent where to place
> And speak in public with some sort of grace.

The scope these lines offer is immense. The first four lines can explore the 'pen is mightier than the sword' in a variety of ways, and the fifth line brings up the whole question of the place of poetry in the lives of young children. Certainly Pope is more than justified in stressing the 'song' quality here, since nothing appeals to children more than the swing of rhythmic verse whatever its subject-matter, a point to be referred to later in the chapter.

The reference to 'teaching a foreigner the tongue' is also most apt, since many people have acquired useful vocabularies and the rudiments of grammar by the memorising of simple poems in another language, and these could well be included in a reading for further variety.

Elsewhere in the work Pope states:

> Yes, sir, reflect, the mischief is not great;
> These madmen never hurt the Church or state;
> Sometimes the folly benefits mankind;
> And rarely avarice taints the tuneful mind.
> Allow him but his plaything of a pen,
> He ne'er rebels, or plots, like other men;
> Flights of cashiers, or mobs, he'll never mind;
> And knows no losses while the Muse is kind.

The character of a poet, his single-mindedness, his few physical needs, his lifelong love affair with his 'Muse' – all these factors have been written about in every period, and poems chosen to illustrate these points can cover many styles and periods as well as being on varying levels according to the age, experience or knowledge of the audience.

Selection of material is one of the great hazards of programme planning since a programme which can completely mystify one section of the public can seem utterly trivial to another. Nowhere is the limitation of language more apparent! One can be told an audience is 'knowledgeable' only to find that their knowledge consists of a few anthology poems remembered from school days and usually late nineteenth century or Georgian. To present such an audience with a programme of complex contemporary material requiring a high degree of concentration and involvement can put them off poetry for life. Conversely to 'entertain' in a polished and urbane way an audience of seriously involved enthusiasts can reduce the whole subject to the level of a drawing-room 'recital'. The former is perhaps preferable to the latter, but to avoid these dilemmas it is wise to discover as much as possible about one's audience and then to be flexible in presentation and always to have alternative poems to offer should the atmosphere appear to warrant it. Thus it has been possible for the lines of Pope already quoted to form the framework for programmes on quite different levels which can yet be equally successful.

The manner of the speaker needs to be flexible too. The same programme can be offered to quite different audiences and be perfectly acceptable if the speaker's own manner accords with the audience's own approach. Thus in a grammar or high school, the approach is generally academic and educational and the speaker can modify both commentary and delivery to suit. Secondary modern and comprehensive schools tend to approach the art subjects more from a feeling of enjoyment and refreshment, and this also can be incorporated in the visiting speaker's presentation. Art festivals are, or should be, 'festive' occasions, theatres theatrical, drama societies dramatic, and so on. This is not 'playing down' or being untrue to oneself, but merely adopting a maxim well known to teachers, that of approaching through what is known to what is not known, and attempting to transmit on a common wavelength through which communication can flow.

Yet it is also a fact that one fixed programme will not, generally speaking, suit varying audiences and situations without some adaptation or modification. This is perhaps because more is required of the listener in a poetry reading than is required of an audience at a play, and a reading has more in common with a 'lesson' than an 'entertainment'. Most teachers would agree that every prepared lesson needs adapting even if only slightly for different classes, and actors or teachers giving poetry readings need to be aware of the variability of circumstances, and be prepared to adjust accordingly.

The most difficult and yet perhaps the most rewarding audience of all are the young or the very young, the infant and primary school children. Their attention must be captured at once and held throughout. They must be approached with seriousness and yet with a sense of shared enjoyment. The manner should be friendly without being too 'cosy', direct without being dictatorial and sound should dominate sense. Here the speaker's voice is of paramount importance since through his tone he can suggest atmosphere and mood, and speaker and listeners can be on common ground. Once a too-intellectual approach begins to intrude, the channel of communication will become blocked and the listeners will begin to feel left behind and rightly resentful. Unlike adults, they will not sit passively waiting for the mysterious language to end and normality return, they will manifest their displeasure as only children can. Again this does not mean playing down, but searching to find worth-while poems which are simple in construction, direct in thought, rhythmical in form, and worthy of attention at any age.

It would be invidious to offer lists of poems which seem to succeed since so much depends on the speaker's own preference and his abilities as interpreter, but experience has shown that poems written especially for children tend to be less successful than poems of true simplicity written for humanity at large. As Coleridge said: 'Children are less than innocent. It is the wishful-thinking adult who imposes on childhood the limitations of extreme innocence.'

To quote Henry James in the preface to *What Maisie Knew*:

> Small children have many more perceptions than they have terms to translate them; their vision is at any moment richer, their apprehension constantly stronger even than their prompt, their at all producible vocabulary.

Thus discussion with children after a poetry reading should be kept to a minimum. A speaker will know only too well where he succeeded and where he failed to hold full interest. Much may have been absorbed, but the children will not possess the vocabulary to develop or discuss their own responses too deeply. Better to let them paint a picture of what they most remember or write a poem or story of their own according to age and intelligence. Sometimes the pictures and poems are in themselves salutary to the reader and a guide to future programmes.

As vocabulary grows (and listening to poetry is one way of assuring that it does) they may require to discuss their preferences and will do so with ease and confidence if early probing has not inhibited them. Poetry can be a living thing to a child and he does not always require his impressions to be translated into language. For example, a D-stream girl of 13 years once asked to 'see' the poem 'Eve' by Ralph Hodgson, after hearing it read. When shown the printed page she said with disappointment, 'Oh! I thought it was a picture.' This would seem to make a good case for letting poetry be *heard* long before it is *seen*. As William Walsh says in *The Use of Imagination*: 'If images initiate understanding, words complete it.'

Without suggesting in any sentimental way that children have an instinctive good taste, it is noticeable how a handful of poems can be gathered which will invariably succeed with generation after generation. Sometimes these seem unbearably hackneyed to the speaker or teacher, yet, examined afresh in the light of a new group, they can frequently be revealed again to the adult as to the child, while a child's own reading can sometimes give exciting insight into over-familiar words. For instance, the 23rd Psalm, spoken with utter confidence by a small boy, came out as:

> The Lord is *my* shepherd,
> *I* shall not want . . .

spoken in a tone of 'Blow you, Jack, I'm all right'.

If a teacher has an ability to speak poetry, it can often be a channel through which he will reach his pupils in a way not perhaps possible in his other classes. A shared experience is, after all, an excellent way of setting up communication. Certainly there should be a sharing in every poetry class, and the reader or teacher is wise to encourage children to join in either by reading their own poems or the poems they like, or by assisting in the chorus of ballads or on-the-spot memorising of simple poems and speaking them altogether. Active participation is a feature of progressive education, though it is to be hoped that the art of *listening* will not be completely neglected since those not trained to listen will miss one whole area of intellectual and emotional stimulus and will be the poorer for it.

As Chapter 7 pointed out, the modern trend in both theatre and education is towards this combined effort on the part of performer and audience, teacher and class – a unity in which all are groping towards an elusive 'truth'. Poetry too needs an intimate and informal atmosphere and a unity of approach from speaker and listener. In most circumstances small groups physically close to the reader are more likely to succeed than remote readings delivered from a high platform, and this should encourage student-readers since it reduces the necessity for vocal projection. In any case, a great deal of poetry is intimate in content and therefore very difficult to convey over vast distances without the aid of a microphone.

On the subject of microphones there is this to be said. The instrument is deplored by many voice experts, yet it has its place and used sensitively it can allow communication to large numbers in acoustically ill-equipped halls and it is a necessity in poetry and jazz. The microphone has also become an integral part of modern 'pop' music. This fact is also deplored by those who remember the powerfully projected voices of the old music hall artists. But to complain of modern inventions is not constructive. We must learn to use them to our advantage. Some of the subtleties of the human voice must be lost when it is amplified by mechanical means, and whenever possible readers will do without it. But if presented with a large audience, and there is any danger of having to use only dramatic or declamatory material as a result, or to run the risk of being inaudible, then surely to refuse a microphone's assistance is idiotic. Also young people feel some bond with a speaker using a microphone, since this is something to which they are accustomed. If this fact alone encourages them to listen to poetry, then that is its justification. In any case, amplification techniques are improving all the time, and the wise speaker will learn to use all modern aids as one more step towards better communication.

Summarising the preparation of programmes. It is necessary to work for unity within the given length and framework but to offer variety in content, length, mood and rhythm, presenting contrasting viewpoints to avoid over-personalising the reading. Titles should be wide-ranging to obviate a too-rigid choice or inferior selection, and care taken in the placing to see that context does not distort the poem's inner meaning.

Permissions and copyright must govern choice, but where possible modern poems should be presented for their immediacy of language and topicality of subject-matter. Poetry readings in conjunction with one-act plays can form an effective double bill, and in longer readings one passage can form a theme for the whole, illustrated through the words and viewpoints of other poets. There is a need to discover the type of audience in order to avoid wrong material, and to be flexible in both presentation and delivery. Young children, though the most rewarding, can also be the most difficult and it is wise to offer them poems of strong sound value and simple meaning; poems indeed which have stood the test of time and are within the scope of a child's imagination.

Finally, if this book has managed to show some of the immense scope spoken poetry offers, and to inspire, stimulate and encourage others to explore and experiment for themselves, then it will have succeeded. No one should be daunted no matter how handicapped he may feel himself to be. In fact handicaps to be overcome are often the greatest spur to success, and the 'infinite capacity to take pains' combined with a genuine desire to communicate has never yet been known to fail. It is not suggested that *all* the training discussed is necessary to *all* speakers. Students can take what they feel they need and build their own training systems for themselves and their pupils.

As to the question often asked, how is it that a poet can read memorably without ever having undergone any training at all, and why is his reading often so preferable to that of a trained speaker, the answer is this. A poet inhabits a very special world. It is a world of heightened sensibilities, of more intense living and feeling translated into language. He therefore needs no special training to enter it, though he can sometimes benefit from training in how to communicate it. Ordinary mortals have to fit themselves to enter this world. Like Alice we have to eat the correct amount of cake and drink the exact amount of liquid in order to get ourselves to the right size to be able to enter, not one mysterious garden, but many. This does not happen in six easy lessons. It has to be worked at constantly, and though some poet's world may be revealed in a relatively short time, others can take years to find.

Writing of the organisation of the feelings, so necessary for finding an individuality of style in written language, Professor William Walsh, in *The Use of Imagination*, used the following passage:

> Honesty is the first requirement; to be utterly honest with ourselves is the beginning. Never to gloss or varnish according to the social code, which renders us, finally, spurious in our innermost selves, able only to summon up at roughly appropriate moments, not feelings at all, but 'clues to clichés'. And then by 'listening'. 'Listening' is a word which, in Lawrence as in Wordsworth, bears a great weight of meaning. It includes training an ear attentive to our feelings, a mind capable of understanding them, a will ready to accept them. It includes patience in attending, acuteness in recognising, generosity in admitting. It enfolds within itself references to the faculties which make possible the fruit of real feeling, a complete imaginative experience.

All this applies equally to the art of speaking poetry, summed up finally by Walt Whitman, whose poem 'Vocalism' has supplied the inspiration for earlier chapters:

Vocalism, measure, concentration, determination and the divine power to speak words.

Surely whoever speaks to me in the right voice, him or her I shall follow.
As the water follows the moon, silently, with fluid steps, anywhere around the globe.

Bibliography

AIKIN, W. A., *The Voice*, Longmans.

ARISTOTLE, *The Art of Poetry* (trans. Bywater, I.), O.U.P.

BELL, J. and BURNISTON, C., *Verbal Dynamics*, Pergamon.

BERRY, F., *Poetry and the Physical Voice*, Routledge.

BIRCH, D., *Training for the Stage*, Pitman.

BROOK, P., *The Empty Space*, MacGibbon.

BRUFORD, R., *Speech and Drama*, Methuen.

BRUFORD, R., *Teaching Mime*, Methuen.

BURNISTON, C., *Speech for Life*, Pergamon.

CHURCH, R., (Ed.), *Poems for Speaking*, Dent.

COBBY, M. and LAURIE, R., *Adventure in Group Speaking*, Bks. 1 and 2, Pitman.

COBBY, M. and LAURIE, R., *Speaking Together*, Pitman.

CRUMP, G., *The Speaking of Poetry*, Dobson Books.

CRUTWELL, B., *The English Sonnet*, Longmans.

DAVY, C., *Words in the Mind*, Chatto.

ELIOT, T. S., *Selected Prose*, Faber.

ESSLIN, M., *Theatre of the Absurd*, Eyre & Spottiswoode.

FRY, R., *Vision and Design*, Chatto.

GARDNER, H., *Business of Criticism*, O.U.P.

GRUBB, F., *A Vision of Reality*, Chatto.

GULLAN, M., *Choral Speaking*, Methuen.

GULLAN, M., *Spoken Poetry in the Schools*, Methuen.

GULLAN, M., and SANSOM, C., *The Poet Speaks*, Methuen.

HARVEY, B., *The Scope of Oracy*, Pergamon.

HENDERSON, A. M., *Good Speaking*, Pan.

HERRIGEL, E., *Zen in the Art of Archery*, Routledge.

IYENGAR, B. K. S., *Light on Yoga*, Allen & Unwin.

JACOBSON, M., *Relaxation*, McGraw-Hill.

JOHNSON, G., BURNISTON, C. and BYRNE, J., *Anthology of Spoken Verse and Prose*, Parts 1 and 2, O.U.P.

LANGER, S. K., *Feeling and Form*, Routledge.

MAWER, I., *The Art of Mime*, Methuen.

MUIR, E., *The Estate of Poetry*, Hogarth.

OPIE, I. and P., *The Language and Lore of Schoolchildren*, O.U.P.

POUND, E., *Pavannes and Divisions*, Faber.

RICHARDS, I. A., *Principles of Literary Criticism*, Routledge.

SCULLY, J. (Ed.), *Modern Poets and Modern Poetry*, Collins.
SPENDER, S., *The Making of a Poem*, Hamish.
STEINER, G., *Language and Silence*, Faber.
SWANN, M., *An Approach to Choral Speech*, Macmillan.
SWANN, M., *Many Voices*, Bks. 1, 2 and 3, Macmillan.
TURNER, C., *Voice and Speech*, Pitman.
TYNAN, K., *Curtains*, Longmans.
VALERY, P., *Reflection on Art*, Routledge.
WALSH, W., *The Use of Imagination*, Chatto.
WAY, B., *Development Through Drama*, Longmans.
WISE, A., *Communication in Speech*, Longmans.

Acknowledgements

GRATEFUL acknowledgement is made to the following authors, owners of copyright, publishers and literary agents for poems and extracts from poems and prose to appear in this book. Also to Mrs. Christabel Burniston, Director of the English Speaking Board, for the suggestion that this book should be written, to Irene Mawer and Molly Topliss for teaching me all I know, and to all those colleges, universities, schools and art festivals who have had the courage to take a chance with an 'unknown' and without whom this experience could never have been gained.

Chatto & Windus Ltd. and Barnes & Noble Inc. for *The Use of Imagination* by William Walsh.

Routledge & Kegan Paul Ltd. for *Feeling and Form* by Susanne K. Langer.

Chatto & Windus Ltd. and Harvard University Press for *Words in the Mind* by Charles Davy.

Frederick Grubb for an extract from his essay 'Poetry and Humanism' in *Poetry Review*, later published in *A Vision of Reality*, Chatto, 1965.

Wesleyan University Press and Jonathan Cape Ltd., publishers, and Mrs. H. M. Davies for 'Leisure' from *The Collected Poems* of W. H. Davies.

Faber & Faber Ltd. and Harcourt, Brace & World Inc. for 'East Coker' from *Four Quartets* and Methuen & Co. Ltd. for an essay 'Tradition and the Individual Talent' from *The Sacred Wood* by T. S. Eliot.

Faber & Faber Ltd. for an extract reprinted from *Pavannes and Divisions* from *Literary Essays of Ezra Pound*.

Faber & Faber Ltd. for 'Sunday Morning', Copyright 1923 and renewed 1951 by Wallace Stevens, and 'The Idea of Order at Key West', Copyright 1936 by Wallace Stevens and renewed 1964 by Molly Stevens Stephenson; reprinted from *The Collected Poems of Wallace Stevens* by permission of Alfred A. Knopf, Inc.

Routledge & Kegan Paul Ltd. for *Reflection on Art* by Paul Valery.

The Clarendon Press, Oxford, for *Business of Criticism* by Helen Gardner.

Routledge & Kegan Paul Ltd. for *Poetry and the Physical Voice* by Francis Berry.

J. M. Dent & Sons Ltd. for 'Fern Hill' by Dylan Thomas from *Collected Poems*.

Max Reinhardt Ltd. for an extract from the booklet issued to The Royal Shakespeare Theatre Club members in 1963.

Methuen & Co. Ltd. for *The Art of Mime* by Irene Mawer.

Jonathan Cape Ltd., the Hogarth Press and Harold Macmillan & Co. Inc., for Sonnets No. 1 and No. 9 from the sequence 'O Dreams O Destinations' by Cecil Day-Lewis from *Collected Poems 1954*.

Routledge & Kegan Paul Ltd. and Harcourt, Brace and World Inc. for *Principles of Literary Criticism* by I. A. Richards.

Faber & Faber Ltd. and Oxford University Press, N.Y. for 'Prayer Before Birth' from *The Collected Poems of Louis MacNeice.*

Faber & Faber Ltd. and Harper Row Inc. for 'Ariel' by Sylvia Plath, © Ted Hughes.

The Marvel Press, Hessle, Yorks. for 'Born Yesterday' by Phillip Larkin reprinted from *The Less Deceived.*

A. P. Watt & Son and Collins–Knowlton–Wing Inc. for 'Warning to Children' by Robert Graves from *Collected Poems 1965* by permission of Robert Graves.

John Murray (Publishers) Ltd. for 'Death in Leamington' by John Betjeman from *Collected Poems.*

Rupert Hart-Davies for 'Timothy Winters' by Charles Causley from *Union Street.*

George Allen & Unwin Ltd. for 'Delicate John' and 'Seascape' from *Little Johnney's Confession* by Brian Patten.

The Hogarth Press Ltd., Mrs. Willa Muir and Harvard University Press for *The Estate of Poetry* by Edwin Muir.

Faber & Faber Ltd. for *Language and Silence* by George Steiner.

Eyre & Spottiswoode Ltd. and Doubleday & Co. Inc. for quotations by Samuel Beckett and Ionesco from *The Theatre of the Absurd* by Martin Esslin.

George Allen & Unwin Ltd. for *Light on Yoga* by B. K. S. Iyengar.

Oxford University Press for *I Remember* by Ann Sexton.

Personal acknowledgement is made to Mr. Vernon Scannell for permission to quote the whole of 'The Lady and the Gypsy'; Mrs. Myfanwy Thomas for 'The Gallows' by Edward Thomas; Mr. John A. Harvey for 'The Fruit is Swinging'; Mr. John Smith for three jazz poems 'He ran out Crying', 'Leaping Dance of Death' and 'Song Before Sunrise'; Mr. John Smith and Rupert Hart-Davies for permission to quote 'A True Story' and 'At The World's End'; Mr. Leonard Clark for permission to quote from his article in *Poetry Review*, and for his constant help and encouragement over the last six years.